EUL VERLAG

EINZELSCHRIFTEN

Ilja Konoplev
Corporate Financial Hedging – Auswirkungen auf die Bewertung und Kreditqualität eines Unternehmens am Beispiel der Lufthansa AG
Lohmar – Köln 2010 ◆ 200 S. ◆ € 49,- (D) ◆ ISBN 978-3-8441-0016-7

Wolf Hoffmann
Turnaround Equity – Erfolgsfaktoren im Transaktionsprozess bei Turnaround-Investitionen in Deutschland
Lohmar – Köln 2011 ◆ 256 S. ◆ € 57,- (D) ◆ ISBN 978-3-8441-0017-4

Christoph Zulehner
Strategisches Führen in Gesundheits- und Pflegeunternehmen – Handbuch für die Praxis
Lohmar – Köln 2011 ◆ 272 S. ◆ € 35,- (D) ◆ ISBN 978-3-8441-0018-1

Mirko Mertenskötter
Qualität, Vertrauen und Akzeptanz im Kontext der Internen Revision
Lohmar – Köln 2011 ◆ 368 S. ◆ € 64,- (D) ◆ ISBN 978-3-8441-0019-8

Jan Breitweg
Planung, Finanzierung und Management von Kunstfonds – Eine empirische Analyse
Lohmar – Köln 2011 ◆ 252 S. ◆ € 57,- (D) ◆ ISBN 978-3-8441-0027-3

Patrick Kraus
Die Auswirkung von Corporate Governance und Nachhaltigkeit auf den Unternehmenserfolg – Eine Betrachtung im Kontext der wertorientierten Unternehmensführung
Lohmar – Köln 2011 ◆ 176 S. ◆ € 48,- (D) ◆ ISBN 978-3-8441-0028-0

Dennis Schlegel
Subsidiary Controlling with Strategically Aligned Performance Measurement Systems
Lohmar – Köln 2011 ◆ 140 S. ◆ € 43,- (D) ◆ ISBN 978-3-8441-0030-3

JOSEF EUL VERLAG

Dennis Schlegel

Subsidiary Controlling with Strategically Aligned Performance Measurement Systems

EUL VERLAG

Bibliografische Information der Deutschen Nationalbibliothek

Die Deutsche Nationalbibliothek verzeichnet diese Publikation
in der Deutschen Nationalbibliografie; detaillierte bibliografische
Daten sind im Internet über <http://dnb.d-nb.de> abrufbar.

ISBN 978-3-8441-0030-3
1. Auflage April 2011

© JOSEF EUL VERLAG GmbH, Lohmar – Köln, 2011
Alle Rechte vorbehalten

JOSEF EUL VERLAG GmbH
Brandsberg 6
53797 Lohmar
Tel.: 0 22 05 / 90 10 6-6
Fax: 0 22 05 / 90 10 6-88
E-Mail: info@eul-verlag.de
http://www.eul-verlag.de

Bei der Herstellung unserer Bücher möchten wir die Umwelt schonen. Dieses
Buch ist daher auf säurefreiem, 100% chlorfrei gebleichtem, alterungsbestän-
digem Papier nach DIN 6738 gedruckt.

Foreword

Performance measurement evolved from various improvement methods, e.g. Total Quality Management, just in time production, Business Engineering. At the very early stage of performance management tools like performance pyramid, Quantum-Performance-Measurement-Model, the French Tableau de Bord and of course Kaplan's and Norton's Balanced Scorecard appeared on the market. Nowadays the Balanced Scorecard probably is the most common tool fulfilling the needs of management and measurement.

Academics emphasise the importance of including non-financial measures. However, surveys among German small and medium sized companies (more than 90% of all companies in Europe belong to that category) show that only about 10% of them actually are using a performance measurement system not only focussing on financial measures.

Consequently, Dennis Schlegel addresses known problems and pitfalls in financial performance measures instead of merely judging them to be inadequate as other authors on performance measurement do. Moreover, he emphasises the importance of aligning controlling systems with strategy and other situational variables. He uses contingency theory as a methodological framework for doing so.

The originality of the thesis is especially originated in the fact that he brings together Anglo-Saxon literature on performance measurement with German literature on subsidiary controlling. Also, he discusses issues that occur in the intersection of the two topics such as the aggregation of value-based measures or the estimation of divisional cost-of-capital.

Prof. Dr. Bernd Britzelmaier

Preface

As the size and importance of company groups is growing, the question how subsidiaries and divisions can be controlled effectively is becoming more and more relevant. The probably most important tool for doing so in practice is performance measurement and management. The basic idea behind performance measurement systems is setting quantitative targets for financial and non-financial performance measures and remunerating responsible managers according to the degree to which they fulfil these targets.

In this thesis, the concept of performance measurement systems in general is explained and particularities in the context of subsidiary controlling are addressed. On the one hand, financial performance measures are discussed in detail. On the other hand, it is emphasised that performance measurement systems have to be adapted to the characteristics of the respective company. It is attempted to give concrete guidance on how the components of performance measurement systems should be designed depending on certain variables such as strategy, organisational structure or size. The objective of this thesis is to be relevant for practice and at the same time theoretically and empirically well-founded.

This thesis was the completion and highlight of my Master's studies in Controlling, Finance & Accounting and at the same time a preparation for my PhD research. I would like to take the opportunity to thank everybody that has supported and encouraged me on my way so far – especially Prof. Dr. Bernd Britzelmaier and my parents.

I am grateful for criticism, comments and questions concerning my work.

Dennis Schlegel

Outline of contents

Table of contents

List of figures

List of abbreviations

β	Equity beta factor
σ	Standard deviation / volatility
μ	Expected return
ASR	Adjusted Sharpe ratio
BSC	Balanced Scorecard
CAPM	Capital Assets Pricing Model
CF	Cash flow
CFROI	Cash Flow Return on Investment
$CFROI_{mod}$	Modified Cash Flow Return on Investment
CGU	Cash generating unit
COC	Cost of capital
COE	Cost of equity
cov	Covariance
cp.	Compare
CV	Company value
CVA	Cash Value Added
D_t	Dividend at time t
Div	Dividend
DCF	Discounted cash flow
dr	Differential return
e.g.	exempli gratia *(for example)*
EPS	Earnings per share
EVA	Economic Value Added
F.	Framework
GCF	Gross cash flow
GCI	Gross cash investment
HGB	Handelsgesetzbuch
i.e.	id est *(that is)*
IAS	International Accounting Standard
IFRS	International Financial Reporting Standard(s)
IRR	Internal rate of return
jα	Jensen's alpha

KPI	Key performance indicator
MIS	Management information system
MVA	Market Value Added
NA	Net assets
NOPAT	Net operating profit after tax
OLAP	Online analytical processing
P_0	Price at time 0
P_t	Price at time t
PMS	Performance measurement system
PV	Present value
R	Actual return
r	Return
r_f	Risk-free rate of return
R&D	Research and development
REVA	Refined Economic Value Added
ROCE	Return on capital employed
ROI	Return on investment
RONA	Return on net assets
SBU	Strategic business unit
SME	Small and medium-sized enterprises
SR	Sharpe ratio
SV	Shareholder value
TR	Treynor ratio
U.K.	United Kingdom
U.S.	United States of America
var	Variance
VBM	Value-based management
WACC	Weighted average cost of capital

1 Introduction

1.1 Topicality and literature review

Subsidiary controlling is a crucial task in today's enterprises. There is a variety of reasons why this topic is and will continue being important – among others the growing importance and complexity of company groups, an increasingly dynamic environment and the proceeding decentralisation in company groups as a result to an increased need for flexibility (Horváth 2006, p. 541; Littkemann 2009, p. 3; Langfield-Smith, Thorne & Hilton 2009, p. 542).

Performance measurement systems (PMS) are a key instrument of subsidiary controlling. The correct use of performance measures combined with incentives can help reduce information asymmetry between the corporate centre and subsidiaries and at the same time ensure an orientation at corporate objectives on all levels.

Subsidiary controlling is a relatively new topic, exclusively discussed in Germany. Towards the end of the 1990s, the topic seems to have aroused increasing interest resulting in the publication of a number of dissertations since the turn of the millennium.[1] In the last years, also a few textbooks on the topic have been published.[2] In contrast, theory and empirical research on PMS is dominated by Anglo-Saxon publications. They date back until the 1970s/1980s.[3] Mostly, holistic concepts with a focus on strategy and non-financial measures are discussed on a very abstract level. It can furthermore be noticed that the topics subsidiary controlling and PMS are normally dealt with separately from each other.

---

[1] For example Borchers (2000), Meier (2001), Faul (2004) or Schumacher (2005).

[2] For example Burger & Ulbrich (2005) or Krupp (2007).

[3] For example Otley (1980).

1.2 Objectives, proceeding and scope

The **objective** of this thesis is to point out how subsidiaries can be controlled with the help of integrated PMS. It is operated under the premise of shareholder value maximisation. Therefore, principles of *value-based management (VBM)* will be outlined briefly as well.

The topic is going to be dealt with in a *contingency approach*, i.e. it is intended to show how PMS are supposed to be designed depending on certain internal and external contextual factors such as environmental uncertainty, business strategy or the size of a company.

In contrast to most publications on PMS, the focus will be on *financial measures*. This includes the discussion of categories of measures, particularities in the calculation for subsidiaries and a thorough examination of known problems of financial measures (dysfunctions and biases). Instead of merely denouncing financial measures, it will be shown if and how these problems can be relieved.

An *integrative approach* will be presented: The sub-topics subsidiary controlling, PMS and VBM which are usually discussed separately from each other are going to be integrated. Moreover, German and international literature will be used in order to benefit from a larger body of knowledge. Additionally, concepts from both economics and business administration will be included as well as concepts from its sub-disciplines finance and (managerial) accounting.

The aspiration of this thesis is to provide a *practice-oriented* guidance which is at the same time *theoretically* well-founded. Also, findings from *empirical* research will be included.

The **structure** of the thesis is outlined in Figure 1. In chapter 2, the used terminology is defined and the conceptual foundation is laid which will be needed in the subsequent chapters.

The structure of chapters 3 to 5 follows the framework for PMS design suggested by Neely, Gregory & Platts (1995, p. 81) which comprises three levels of analysis: The individual performance measures (level 1), PMS as an entity (level 2) and the relationship between PMS and its environment (level 3). The discussion of performance measures in chapter 3 will be limited to financial performance measures whereas the other chapters refer to PMS in general. In chapter 4, the applied contingency methodology will be explained thoroughly, before general questions of PMS design will be addressed. In chapter 5, contextual factors will be identified and it will be shown how they influence the design of PMS. On each level, particularities of subsidiary controlling are included.

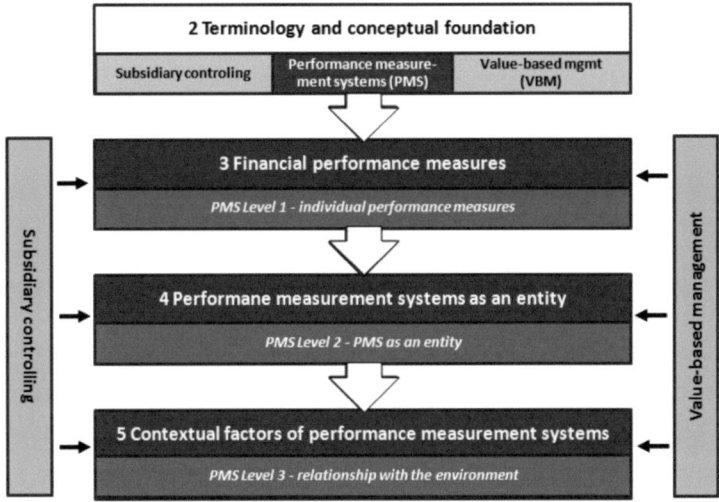

Figure 1: Structure of the thesis
Source: Own illustration

The thesis is written from the point of view of the corporate centre of a multi-business company group. The following topics are excluded from the **scope** of this thesis: The discussion of individual non-financial measures, taxation and transfer pricing issues and the process of implementing a PMS.

2 Terminology and conceptual foundation

2.1 Subsidiary controlling

2.1.1 Delineation of subsidiary controlling and overview

As subsidiary controlling is a relatively new topic, no standard definition has established itself yet (Borchers 2006, pp. 233-234)[4]. In this thesis the following definition is used: *Subsidiary controlling is the coordination and control of subsidiaries, oriented towards the overall objectives of the company group (corporate objectives).*[5] In the following chapters the elements included in the definition – the need for coordination, the definition of subsidiary and the objectives of company groups – will be specified more in detail.

The term *subsidiary controlling* also has to be distinguished from *company group controlling*: Also for this distinction, different and contradictory statements can be found in literature (Burger & Ulbrich 2005, p. 86). Here, the distinction is made by means of the following two differences: First, company group controlling is directed towards the company group as a whole (including the corporate centre) while subsidiary controlling focuses on individual subsidiaries (Kremer 2008, p. 62; Borchers 2000, p. 57). Second, company group controlling requires the affiliation of subsidiaries with a company group (Borchers 2006, p. 238) while broad definitions of subsidiary controlling also include the controlling of shares in companies which cannot be classified as part of the company group, for instance ones that are in the process of acquisition.

Latter point is related to the concept of a *subsidiary life cycle*: It can be divided into acquisition phase, operating phase and divestment phase (Huch, Behme & Ohlendorf 2004, p. 443). More recent publications in-

---

[4] As even controlling in general is a comparably controversial topic in German-speaking literature, it is questionable if a standard definition will emerge soon.

[5] The definition includes common elements of several definitions from literature. For an overview cp. (Littkemann 2009, p. 10).

clude 'integration' as a fourth phase, located between acquisition phase and operating phase (Krupp 2007, p. 37; Burger & Ulbrich 2005, p. 10). Subsidiaries according to the definition of this thesis are typically in their operating phase. Depending on the phase in the lifecycle, there is a different focus of subsidiary controlling (Borchers 2006, p. 241). In the operating phase, important tasks are planning and control as well as coordination of the subsidiaries in terms of the corporate objectives (Krupp 2007, p. 37).

Subsidiary controlling can be seen from different perspectives. The *institutional perspective* examines organisational aspects. On the one hand, this refers to structural aspects such as if there is a special department in charge of subsidiary controlling and where in the organisation it is located. On the other hand, the competences of central and local controlling are discussed (Meier 2001, pp. 42-44). The *functional perspective* addresses activities which are supposed to be undertaken by subsidiary controlling in order to ensure the achievements of objectives (Kremer 2008, p. 68). The *instrumental perspective* focuses on methods, models and techniques for the realisation of subsidiary controlling activities (Meier 2001, p. 41). They can be classified into personal, technocratic and structural instruments. In practice, the emphasis is on technocratic instruments, especially reporting and value-based instruments such as value-based performance measures (Borchers 2006, p. 245; Meier 2001, pp. 41-42).

As an intermediate summary, it can be said that this thesis adopts an instrumental view on the controlling of subsidiaries that are in their operating phase and included in a company group. In definitional terms, the topic is a special case of *subsidiary controlling in company groups* rather than company group controlling as the controlling of the corporate centre is excluded.

2.1.2 Objects of subsidiary controlling

As stated above, the objects of subsidiary controlling are subsidiaries that form part of a company group. There are several ways to define what a **company group** is. In particular it can be distinguished between a legal and an economic point of view. Legally, especially consolidated financial accounting regulations could be referred to. In this thesis, a company group is defined as an enterprise that consists of *one central top-level entity ('corporate centre') and several local lower-level entities ('subsidiaries')*. There are a number of different possibilities to demarcate subsidiaries as shown in the subsequent paragraph. The top-level entity can be active on the market. However, there is a trend towards *holding companies,* i.e. towards top-level entities whose main purpose is the management of lower-level entities. Additionally there can be several intermediate holding companies which comprise several lower-level entities (Faul 2004, pp. 47-49; Hüllmann 2003, pp. 17-19; Bleicher 1991, p. 630).

Concerning the demarcation of **subsidiaries**, two questions have to be regarded: First, how the local entities can be demarcated from each other for the purpose of controlling, i.e. for instance for a separate performance measurement (see no. 1 in Figure 2). Second, which local entities are subsidiaries in the meaning of this thesis, i.e. form part of the company group (see no. 2 in Figure 2).

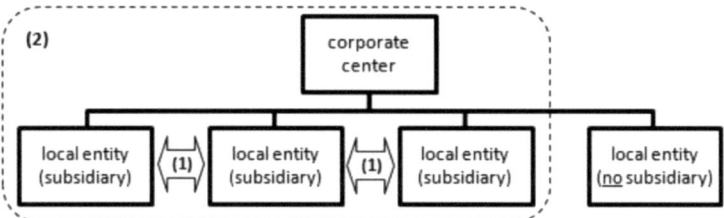

Figure 2: Demarcation of subsidiaries
Source: Own illustration

(1) Demarcation of local entities

The primary structure of a company group is determined by the legal ownership structure. However, this statutory structure is overlaid by an operational structure in so-called *dual organisations* (Borchers 2006, pp. 240-241). As mentioned above, the relevant point of view for the purpose of this thesis is economic, i.e. the operational structure is relevant. A division of an enterprise might for instance have the same economic characteristics as a legally independent subsidiary of another enterprise.

Burger & Ulbrich (2005, pp. 95-96) propose aligning legal and operational structure which has several advantages. Above all, financial data is primarily available from financial accounting, i.e. oriented towards the legal structure. Moreover, split-offs of subsidiaries are easier. However, a virtual organisation is more flexible than a permanent adjustment of the legal structure and the problem of data availability can be solved by an additional assignment of posts in the accounting system to profit centres (Borchers 2006, p. 241).

But also from an economic point of view there are several ways to subdivide a company group. Vogel (1998, pp. 90-91) names minimum requirements which should be fulfilled for the demarcation of subsidiaries in the context of value-based management (so-called value centres): It must be possible to valuate them separately, i.e. cash flows (CF) and cost-of-capital must be separately identifiable. Moreover, they must be lead by managers with competences and responsibility for the task of value creation.

It is conceivable to use two existing concepts for the demarcation: First, the concept of a *cash generating unit (CGU)* from the International Financial Reporting Standards (IFRS) which is used for impairment tests could be applied. A CGU is "the smallest identifiable group of assets that generates cash inflows that are largely independent of the cash inflows from other assets" (IAS 36.6). Second, the concept of a *strategic business unit*

(SBU) as defined in strategic marketing could be used. A SBU is a product-market combination which is strategically independent from other SBUs (Huch, Behme & Ohlendorf 2004, p. 445).

This thesis adopts the concept of SBUs due to two reasons: First, there are certain instruments of subsidiary controlling which are based on SBUs, e.g. portfolio models. Second, in the planning and control process, performance targets are to be derived from strategic goals so that a strategic demarcation of subsidiaries is required. Moreover, it is assumed that SBUs fulfil the definition of a CGU anyways.

As the question of how to demarcate subsidiaries is actually an organisational question, the demarcation of objects of subsidiary controlling, i.e. for internal control, should be consistent with the organisational structure. This also leads to complexities since the operational structure is often multi-dimensional in modern companies. *Matrix organisations*, for instance with a functional, a product-oriented and a regional dimension are common in contemporary company groups. Thus, also multidimensional performance measurement according to the respective responsibilities has to be done.

In the context of controlling decentralised entities, the concept of *responsibility centre organisations* is often referred to. Depending on the extent to which responsibility is transferred and on the measures according to which the centre managers are evaluated, it is distinguished between cost centres, expense centres, revenue centres and investment centres. Latter is the strongest form of decentralisation. Managers of investment centres are evaluated based on value-based measures, i.e. invested capital is taken into account in addition to profit (Jensen & Meckling 2009, pp. 50-55; Faul 2004, pp. 42-43). Subsidiaries as defined in this thesis are regularly profit or investment centres.[6]

---

[6] This is also consistent with the type of performance measures presented in chapter 3.

(2) Inclusion of local entities in the company group

In this thesis, a local entity is seen as part of the company group and thus as a subsidiary if the following two criteria are applicable. Such subsidiaries should be in the range of application of the performance measurement system. First, the local entity is under the *uniform management*[7] of the company group which means that common objectives are pursued and the corporate centre assumes non-delegatable tasks such as resource allocation (Schmidbauer 1998, pp. 29-31; Faul 2004, p. 47). Second, the corporate centre can (but not necessarily does) actively influence and integrate the local entity's strategy (Schumacher 2005, pp. 60-61; Horváth 1997, p. 82; Maier 2001, p. 44). Whether the influence is based on shares in the company, contracts or other factors is irrelevant from an economic point of view (Maier 2001, p. 44).

2.1.3 Economic framework conditions and necessity

In practice, the **importance of company groups** is very high. There are a number of economic concepts and reasons which can explain the existence and emergence of large company groups, for instance the realisation of economies of scope (synergy effects) and economies of scale as well as acquisitions as a growth strategy (Burger & Ulbrich 2005, p. 51; Faul 2004, p. 44; Krupp 2007, p. 1).

As a result to increased organisational size and complexity, a growing divisionalisation can be observed among large companies (Horváth 2006, p. 541). Divisionalisation refers to companies being comprised of multiple responsibility centres. It is a form of **decentralisation**, i.e. a form of delegating decisions and tasks to lower hierarchical levels (Merchant & Van der Stede 2007, p. 445; Schumacher 2005, p. 68; Faul 2004, p. 39). Motives for a decentralisation are above all an increased flexibility for subsidiaries to react to market demands, to reduce the work load of the corporate centre's management and motivational effects due to increased re-

---

[7] *German: Einheitliche Leitung*

sponsibility and freedom of subsidiary managers (Schumacher 2005, p. 68; Faul 2004, p. 40).

Decentralisation raises the question how the orientation towards corporate objectives can still be ensured on all organisational levels(Horváth 2006, p. 10). This problem can be described with the help of the **principal agent problem** which is a concept from New Institutional Economics (Schmidbauer 1998, p. 45). A principal agent relationship is a "contract under which one or more persons (the principal(s)) engage another person (the agent) to perform some service on their behalf which involves delegating some decision making authority to the agent" (Jensen & Meckling 1976, p. 308). The relationship is assumed to have the following characteristics: First, the principal's and the agent's *interests are divergent* and the *agent acts opportunistically*, i.e. is likely to misuse the delegated authority for his own benefit. Second, the agent is able to enforce his own interests, since there is *information asymmetry* in favour of the agent (Weber & Schäffer 2006, p. 25). This creates a reduction of the principal's welfare which can be classified as different types of agency costs (Jensen & Meckling 1976, p. 308).

The problem is general in nature and can be applied to a number of different circumstances. In company groups it exists in the relationship between shareholders and top management due to the separation of ownership and control. Furthermore, it exists at every level within the company group (Jensen & Meckling 1976, p. 309). This creates principal agent relationships with multiple tiers as for instance the group management is the subsidiary management's principal and the shareholders' agent at the same time (Scharfstein & Stein 2000, p. 2541). The information asymmetry created by decentralisation is actually intended (specialisation) but creates the principal agent problem. This implies that there must be an optimal degree of decentralisation (Faul 2004, p. 133).

From a functional point of view, these economic framework conditions highlight the need for coordination as included in the definition of subsidiary controlling in order to ensure that the agents hold on to the corporate objectives.

2.2 Performance measurement systems

2.2.1 Delineation, purposes and elements

Even though performance measurement is a widely discussed topic, only few authors make an attempt to sharply define the term (Schreyer 2007, p. 28). Moreover, the term is used for a variety of different concepts in business and economics ranging from securities and portfolio analysis[8] to manufacturing controlling[9]. Thus it is indispensable at this point to clearly delineate the term performance measurement as it is used in this thesis.

First of all, *performance* itself has to be discussed. While Lebas and Euske (2007) provide a comprehensive discussion of the general meaning of the word, here only the relevant characteristics for businesses will be mentioned. Grünig (2002, pp. 4-5) defines performance as the capability of a company to reach its goals. Furthermore, it is often stated that performance has two fundamental dimensions: effectiveness and efficiency of actions (Neely, Gregory & Platts 1995, pp. 80-81).[10]

Following this notion of performance, a *performance measure* can be defined as a metric used to quantify the efficiency or effectiveness of an action. Consequently, *performance measurement* is the process of quantifying the efficiency and effectiveness of actions (Neely, Gregory & Platts 1995, pp. 80-81; Horváth 2006, p. 562).

---

[8] For example Fischer (2001).

[9] For example Tangen (2004).

[10] Effectiveness refers to the achievement of an objective (output only) while efficiency also takes into account the resources (input) required to produce the outcome (Hoque 2003, p. 52).

Neely, Gregory & Platts (Performance measurement system design 1995, pp. 80-81) define *performance measurement system (PMS)* as a set of metrics used to quantify both the efficiency and effectiveness of actions. In this thesis, however, the term is defined more broadly. Here, a PMS not only includes the set of metrics, but also the planning and control process in which targets for the performance measures are set (cp. chapter 2.2.2), the incentive system attached to the measures (cp. chapter 2.2.3) and the reporting system. Reporting refers to the process of information transmission which is necessary due to the divergence of origin and use of information in decentralised organisations (Horváth 2006, p. 583).

In literature, a large number of purposes and goals of PMS are stated. They can all be related to one of the two basic functions of PMS: *information function* and *behaviour control function* (Ewert & Wagenhofer 2008, p. 521; Schumann 2008, pp. 87-88). On the one hand, PMS convey information from lower levels to top management (bottom-up), but also help communicate the strategy and plans top-down to lower levels (Simons 2000, p. 4; Langfield-Smith, Thorne & Hilton 2009, p. 691). Additionally, they help managers to compare their own performance to previously set targets and to take corrective actions in time (Hoque 2003, p. 142; Otley 1999, p. 369). This enables well-founded management decisions (Bititci, Carrie & McDevitt 1997, p. 524). On the other hand, PMS can be used to control behaviour by monitoring managers' performance and using it as a basis for compensation (Hoque 2003, pp. 142-143). Also, benchmarking between several subsidiaries or with external parties can be done (Burger & Ulbrich 2005, pp. 349-353).

2.2.2 PMS from a systems theory and a process perspective

A **system** consists of elements which are related to one another and have certain attributes (Fuchs 1972, pp. 48-49; König 2005, p. 14). The general definition of a system does not further specify what an element is so that different things can be considered as elements. In particular, elements of one system can be lower-level systems themselves (Fuchs 1972, p. 49).

Thus there is a hierarchy of systems on different levels: the respective system being examined, its super-system(s) and its sub-systems (Horváth 2006, p. 82). The demarcation, i.e. the boundary of the system can be defined depending on the purpose of the analysis (Horváth 2006, p. 82).

General Systems Theory – developed in the 1950s and 1960s – is supposed to be an interdisciplinary theory as the questions examined are relevant in all research disciplines (König 2005, p. 14; Fuchs 1972, p. 48). In business administration it is especially transferred to organisational theory and management control questions.

PMS can be seen as a system which is part of a super-system that comprises performance measurement among other interrelated systems (Neely, Gregory & Platts 1995, p. 102; Hoque 2003, p. 45). In Anglophone literature, the super-system of PMS is frequently referred to as Management Control System (MCS), for instance by Anthony & Govindarajan (2001). Also in German literature, a systems view of management is often adopted – above all by Horváth (2006, p. 81).

Also an organisation as a whole can be considered a system with the external environment being its super-system (Bleicher 1972, p. 236). Organisations are a special type of system which have the following two characteristics (among others): They are open – i.e. there are exchange processes with the wider environment – and they are dynamic (Printz 2008, p. 29; Jackson 2000, p. 110).

So what is the use of systems theory for this thesis? First of all, the attribute of organisations of being open systems emphasises the need to consider relevant contextual factors from the environment. Indeed, contingency theory is based on systems theory (Jackson 2000, pp. 108-110; Staehle, Conrad & Sydow 1999, p. 48). Second, systems theory assumes a holistic view (Fuchs 1972, p. 47) and represents a notion of mutual influence and interdependence between elements (König 2005, p. 15). This shows that interdependences between several elements of PMS and also between PMS and other systems must be considered when conducting research on systems or designing systems (cp. chapter 4.2.1).

In spite of the advantages of systems theory, the downsides should be kept in mind. In particular, the interdisciplinary integration leads to a high abstraction level. That means that the practical applicability might be limited and analogies for instance between biological systems and business organisations should be regarded critically as they might neglect important differences (Staehle, Conrad & Sydow 1999, p. 41; Horváth 2006, p. 88).

By introducing a time dimension (dynamic view), systems can be analysed from a **process** perspective (Horváth 2006, p. 83). The performance measurement process is closely related to the general planning and control process (Gleich 2001, p. 21). Systems theory involves thinking in loops instead of linear processes (König 2005, p. 16). Therefore, with the inclusion of feedback loops, the performance measurement process becomes a cybernetic control loop (Gladen 2008, p. 27; Gleich 2001, p. 21). In Figure 3, the performance measurement process and its connection to the general planning and control process is outlined.

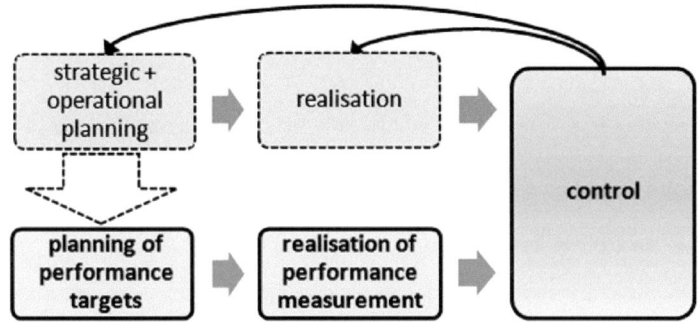

Figure 3: The performance measurement process
Source: Own illustration

Planning of performance targets

PMS compare actual performance with a budgeted target or an external benchmark (Langfield-Smith, Thorne & Hilton 2009, p. 691; Hoque 2003, pp. 142-143; Simons 2000, p. 7). Therefore, as a first step, targets have to be set. In performance measurement literature, it is usually recommended to break down an organisation's strategy and top objectives to individual performance measures. This is an enhancement of classic target planning as performance targets are formulated with reference to persons and objects (Horváth 2006, p. 562). The personalised targets are then linked to incentives which has to be made transparent *beforehand* in order to induce the right behaviour.

Realisation of performance measurement

In this phase, the actual measurement is done, i.e. the performance measures' actual values at a specified point in time are recorded and compared to the target values (Gleich 2001, p. 23). This involves topics such as reporting and information systems.

Control and feedback

The deviations between target and actual values should be analysed in order to trigger an ex post learning process. While in so-called single-loop learning only the realisation of activities is adapted as a result to deviations, double-loop learning involves bringing into question planning premises and strategies (Dittmar 2004, pp. 73-75; Gladen 2008, p. 32). However, it has to be mentioned that in terms of employee motivation and reward, an adaption of the original performance target is problematic.

2.2.3 Incentives as a solution to the principal agent problem

In literature, two main strategies to make employees follow planning and thus reduce agency costs are identified: The first one is *monitoring* management's actions and intervening if necessary. While this can reduce some obvious agency costs such as exaggerated perks, complex decisions such as capital investments cannot be monitored thoroughly due to the information asymmetry involved. Moreover, monitoring is costly and can have a negative impact on motivation of local managers (Burger & Ulbrich 2005, pp. 59-60; Brealey, Myers & Allen 2008, pp. 328-333).

The second strategy is to design compensation plans which give managers the right incentives (Brealey, Myers & Allen 2008, p. 331). The importance of setting positive incentives in order to solve the principal agent problem is considered very high. While monitoring and sanctions can only prevent wrong decision, positive incentives to achieve output-oriented objectives can initiate value-adding decisions (Riegler 2000, p. 152; Faul 2004, p. 134).

An incentive system must reward activities that are in the principal's interest, i.e. increase company value. Thus the principal's and the agent's interests are aligned and do no longer diverge so that the agent acts in the principal's interest by acting in his own interest (Riegler 2000, p. 148; Faul 2004, pp. 134-135). In order that the right behaviour is induced, a correct ex post performance measurement is crucial. As Brealey et al (2008, p. 327) put it: "Since you get what you reward and you reward what you measure, you get what you measure."

2.2.4 Financial vs. non-financial performance measurement

Traditionally, performance measurement focused on financial measures (Langfield-Smith, Thorne & Hilton 2009, p. 691; Schreyer 2007, p. 26). That was until the 1980s when there was a growing realisation that traditional performance measures would no longer fulfil the requirements of new competitive realities such a need for flexibility or rapid response to customer expectations (Kennerley & Neely 2003, p. 214; Chow & Van der Stede 2006, p. 1). Therefore, modern PMS place a greater emphasis on a balance between financial and non-financial measures (Langfield-Smith,

Thorne & Hilton 2009, p. 694).[11] Today, there is a variety of performance measurement concepts. A prominent example is the Balanced Scorecard (BSC) by Kaplan and Norton, but there are also less known concepts such as the Performance Prism by Adams and Neely (Horváth 2006, p. 563).

Financial performance measures have been heavily criticised by academics and practitioners (Langfield-Smith, Thorne & Hilton 2009, pp. 692-694; Neely, Gregory & Platts 1995, p. 106; Tangen 2004, pp. 726-727). The following are often-cited points of criticism:

(1) They describe consequences of decisions and actions, not causes. Therefore, they are not helpful in analysing the past and also provide limited guidance for future action. The reason is that financial measures are highly aggregated while non-financial measures can be broken down to the operational level. Additionally, many issues are difficult to quantify monetarily. Non-financial measures can for instance deal with questions related to customer satisfaction while financial measures do not provide information on what customer desire and what competitors do.

(2) They lack timeliness, i.e. they only display results of decisions with delay.

(3) They lack strategic focus and even may conflict with strategic objectives.

(4) They have an inflexible format which is the same across all departments. However, each department's unique situation should be taken into account.

(5) They encourage sub-optimisation.

(6) They encourage short-termism.

---

[11] Besides the balance between financial and non-financial measures, contemporary PMS include principles such a strategic orientation, external benchmarks or continuous improvement thinking. However, they are not dealt with at this point since this paragraph focuses on *financial vs. non-financial measures* and not *traditional vs. contemporary PMS*.

Despite the weaknesses of financial measures, modern concepts of performance measurement can (of course) not completely renounce on financial measures (Horváth 2006, p. 562). Furthermore, there is a tendency in literature to ignore potential weaknesses of non-financial measures (Chow & Van der Stede 2006, p. 2). Thus it has to be further examined if a blanket judgment against *all* financial measures is justified and if there are possibilities to remedy the weaknesses by improving design or usage of the measures or other parts of the control systems.

Point (1) is surely true to a certain degree. However, the problem is less relevant to subsidiary controlling as it is very deep in the operational level. Point (2) will be included as an evaluation criterion in the discussion of individual measures (chapter 3.1.1). Points (3) and (4) underline the importance of a contingent design of performance measurement systems which will be addressed in chapter 4. Points (5) and (6) will be dealt with in detail in chapter 3.3 under the headline *dysfunctions and biases of financial performance measures*. The term 'measurement dysfunction' means that "the measurement process itself contributes to behaviour contrary to what is in the best interest of the organisation" (Spitzer 2007, p. 22). A bias is a systematic error in measurement that is constantly made since it is not originated in the data but in the measurement design (Dieck 2007, pp. 28-29).

2.3 Value-based management

2.3.1 Shareholder value as a bottom-line goal

As the purpose of a Master's Thesis should not be the reproduction of basic knowledge, the discussion of VBM is limited to the aspects which are needed for the development of concepts in the course of this thesis. However, it is important to clearly define the bottom-line goal of VBM in the sense of this thesis in order to be able to evaluate financial performance measures in terms of their congruence with the top goal.

The intention of VBM is the management and enhancement of the company value (CV) or shareholder value (SV) (Britzelmaier 2009, pp. 13-

15).[12] Shareholder value is the value of a company's equity and defined as $SV = CV - value\ of\ debt$. Hence, CV and SV can be mathematically converted into one another (Matschke & Brösel 2007, pp. 688-89). Assuming a constant debt amount or a constant debt/equity ratio, maximisation of CV and maximisation of SV are complementary goals so that in the following no differentiation between the two goals will be made.

As opposed to the time before the 1960s, today the notion is prevalent that there is no objective value of an asset or a company, but that the correct method to estimate the value depends on the purpose of the valuation (Langguth 2008, pp. 8-10). According to this, it has to be discussed, which valuation method is the functional one for the purpose of internal control of a VBM concept. The three basic valuation methods categories are net asset value-oriented approaches, investment-oriented approaches and market-oriented approaches. It is widely agreed that an investment-oriented view is to be preferred over a net asset value-oriented approach under a going concern assumption (Britzelmaier 2009, p. 21). In investment-oriented approaches, the value corresponds to the present value (PV) of future income. Among the investment-oriented approaches, the discounted cash flow (DCF) method is considered *the* standard investment-oriented method internationally. [13] However, also market-oriented approaches which operate based on observable market capitalisations or

---

[12] While it is often criticised that interest of both shareholders and stakeholders should be taken into account, in this thesis it is assumed that other stakeholders' goals (especially customers' and employees') are implicitly included as a constraint to the maximisation of SV. Sustainable enhancement of CV without consideration of interest of these important stakeholders is not possible.

[13] Ballwieser (2007, p. 9) warns that there are different versions of the DCF method and an "inconsiderate application" does not necessarily lead to equal results. In this thesis the WACC version is used which discounts free cash flows of shareholders *and* debt-holders (entity approach) with the weighted average cost of capital (WACC) (Perridon & Steiner 2007, p. 209). The WACC approach assumes a constant debt/equity-ratio (Matschke & Brösel 2007, p. 674; Perridon & Steiner 2007, p. 210) so that the above-made assumption of complementarity of CV and SV maximisation is met.

recent transaction prices and transfer these to comparable companies with the help of multiples might be adequate.

According to the *efficient markets theory* which reached its height during the 1970s when the concept of rational expectations prevailed in economic theory, all currently available information should be reflected in the stock price (Shiller 2003, p. 83; Wessels 2000, p. 252). If investors' expectations were homogeneous and information complete, all companies would be fairly priced which means that stocks trade at their fundamental (i.e. DCF) value and the required rate of return is the opportunity cost of capital. Otherwise, arbitrage processes would restore equilibrium (McLaney 2006, pp. 252-253; Vogel 1998, p. 93; Brealey, Myers & Allen 2008, p. 363). However, in practice the DCF value of the company does *not* correspond to the market value due to market imperfections such as valuation anomalies (e.g. small firm effect)[14], bubbles, irrationalities in the investors' behaviour and general medium-term cyclical fluctuations of price-earnings ratios (Brealey, Myers & Allen 2008, pp. 363-367; Merchant & Van der Stede 2007, p. 439). Thus the question which of the concepts should be used as a target for VBM remains.

It could be argued that the *market value* is in practice the actual realisation of SV, especially for minority shareholder of publicly owned companies. On the other hand, *DCF approaches* are future-oriented taking into account operating and strategic planning (Vogel 1998, p. 55). Even if markets were efficient, this does not imply that they are perfect, i.e. they can only reflect information that is available. That means that internally known plans, prospects and confidential information – e.g. about research & development – which are extremely important for future income and thus value are *not* included in the market price so that the correct value can

---

[14] It could also be argued that the valuation models – especially the models to determine the opportunity cost of capital – fail in explaining certain effects. Instead of anomalies in the market, the assumed fair value might be calculated incorrectly and the market valuation might be correct.

only be determined by an internal DCF valuation (McLaney 2006, pp. 252-253; Merchant & Van der Stede 2007, p. 439). In this thesis, the fundamental standpoint is represented, arguing that the market value is only a proxy of the intrinsic fundamental value and approximates it in the long-run as internal information is released with delay.

2.3.2 Estimating the cost-of-capital

The cost of capital (COC) is a crucial figure in VBM as a discount rate in valuations and for the use in value-based performance measures. It is calculated as a weighted average cost of capital (WACC) from the expected returns on equity and the actual interest on debt, weighted by their market values [15] (Horváth 2006, p. 485; Brealey, Myers & Allen 2008, p. 241). Thereby, a long-term target capital structure is to be used (Britzelmaier 2009, p. 69; Matschke & Brösel 2007, p. 666).

For the estimation of cost of equity, theoretical capital market models are used. In practice, the use of Lintner (1965) and Sharpe's (1964) *Capital Asset Pricing Model (CAPM)* prevails (Hoffjan 2009, p. 138). According to the CAPM – which builds on Markowitz' (1952) model of portfolio choice – the cost of equity is calculated as follows by adding a risk premium to the risk free rate (e.g. government bonds):

$$r_{equity} = r_f + \beta(r_m - r_f)$$

The risk premium depends on the systematic risk relative to the market portfolio which is the market-related risk of an asset that cannot be diversified. Assets with $\beta = 1$ react to market fluctuation in the same direction and to the same extent as the market portfolio and are hence compensated with the market risk premium $(r_m - r_f)$ in addition to the risk free return r_f (Perridon & Steiner 2007, p. 255; Hoffjan 2009, p. 139). The investor is *not*

---

[15] Market value in this case is meant as opposed to book value, not as opposed to DCF value. In the WACC version of DCF, the equity's DCF value is to be used as weight which leads to the known circularity problem.

compensated for unsystematic risk, i.e. company-individual risk, since it is assumed that it can be diversified away by the investor (Matschke & Brösel 2007, p. 663; Perridon & Steiner 2007, p. 256; Ballwieser 2007, pp. 94-95).

For listed companies, r_m, r_f and β can be estimated ex post from empirical financial market data. For beta this is done by regressing the stock's return against the return of a stock index (Ballwieser 2007, p. 94). The squared correlation coefficient (also called R-squared) can be interpreted as the proportion of the stock's variation which can be explained by the variation of the index, i.e. R-squared is the proportion of systematic risk in the stock's total risk (Brealey, Myers & Allen 2008, pp. 242-244).

$$\beta_{asset,market} = \frac{cov(r_{asset};r_{market})}{var(r_{market})} = \frac{\sigma_{asset}\sigma_{market}\rho_{asset,market}}{\sigma^2_{market}}$$

The CAPM has a very poor empirical record.[16] One reason for that might be the model's many unrealistic simplifying assumptions. However, valid empirical tests are difficult to implement (Fama & French 2004, p. 25). Roll (1977) states in his famous critique that empirical tests might even be in-feasible. Besides criticism concerning extrapolation of past values into the future (Ballwieser 2007, p. 98), another main point of criticism refers to the one-dimensionality of risk factors, so that various multi-dimensional mod-els were proposed, such as the Multi-Beta CAPM by Sharpe himself (Perridon & Steiner 2007, p. 259).

---

[16] Empirical tests are largely based on the following implications of the model: (1) the relation between expected returns and betas is linear and there is no other explanatory factor; (2) beta, i.e. the risk premium is positive; (3) assets that have a beta of zero offer the risk free rate while the risk premium is determined by beta (Fama & French 2004, p. 30). Many studies confirm a positive risk premium. However, returns seem to be flatter than predicted by the CAPM, i.e. returns of low-beta stocks are predicted too low and those of high-beta stocks too high (Fama & French 2004, pp. 43-44; Perridon & Steiner 2007, p. 262).

The probably most discussed multi-dimensional approach is the *Arbitrage Pricing Theory (APT)*. Although its theoretical derivation is different from CAPM, it is also a linear factor model and thus similar in its application (Perridon & Steiner 2007, pp. 263-266):

$$E(r) = r_f + \sum_{k=1}^{K} E(r_{pk} - r_f)\beta_k$$

While the theory itself does not identify any concrete factors (Perridon & Steiner 2007, p. 266), later studies try to find influencing factors empirically.[17] For instance Roll and Ross (1984, p. 14) name inflation, industrial production, risk premiums and the slope of the term structure of interest rates. Fama & French (Common risk factors in the returns on stocks and bonds 1993, p. 3) identify three factors for stocks which are an overall market factor, a factor related to firm size and one related to book-to-market ratio. Brealey, Myers & Allen (2008, p. 221), however, point out that empirical findings could be based on data snooping which is a form of statistical bias. If researchers have not formulated hypotheses in advance, by data mining techniques correlations can be found which have just existed in the past *by chance*.

A different approach is *implied COC*, also called *dividend discount model*. It is based on the notion that the price is equal to discounted dividends.[18] The model uses dividend forecasts and the actual stock price as input variables. The classic formula for a perpetual dividend is solved for the discount factor which is equal to the cost-of-equity (COE) (Britzelmaier 2009, pp. 88-89; Gebhard, Lee & Swaminathan 2001, pp. 140-141).

$$P_0 = \frac{Div}{r_{equity}} \rightarrow r_{equity} = \frac{Div}{P_0}$$

---

[17] Research can be based on factor analysis (which often leads to economically not interpretable results) or on testing preliminarily specified variables (Perridon & Steiner 2007, pp. 266-267).

[18] Cp. the discussion of efficient markets theory above.

This model can be used in several variations, for instance in combination with the CAPM in order to calculate an implied beta (Borgman & Strong 2006, pp. 3-4). While the model is appealing because it is forward-looking and easy to apply, its application within a DCF context would be a circular reasoning. Moreover, it is not compatible with the argumentation of this thesis that the observable stock price differs from the 'real' value of a company.

Despite of its weaknesses, the CAPM seems to have a right of continuance in practice since no alternative model or range of factors for the APT could find a majority, yet. Therefore, the further explanations will be based on the CAPM. Specific issues of the application within the context of subsidiary management and VBM will be discussed in chapter 3.4.

2.4   Relationship between the sub-topics

In this chapter, the connections and overlaps of the three sub-topics of this thesis subsidiary controlling, VBM and PMS will be pointed out in order to locate the topic within the body of knowledge.

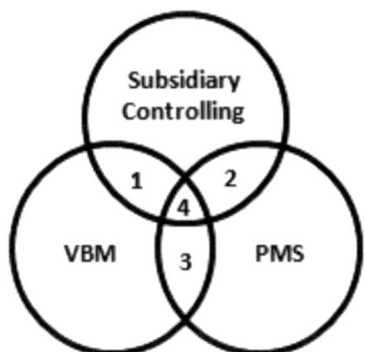

Figure 4: Overlaps of subsidiary controlling, VBM and PMS
Source: Own illustration

(1) VBM and subsidiary management

According to Borchers (2006, p. 234), the recent focus on VBM has lead to a *more active management* of subsidiaries. It should be made sure that all SBUs earn a risk-adequate return on equity. For this purpose there is a variety of instruments, especially portfolio charts which give an overview on all SBUs in terms of their value creation and capital employed (Mittendorfer 2004, pp. 82, 98-100).

The theoretical connection between VBM and subsidiary management is the premise of *value additivity*. The value additivity principle states that the value of two combined CF streams is equal to the sum of their present values (Schaefer 2002, p. 93). By analogy, it is argued that the value of a company group is the sum of the subsidiaries' values. This is used in a valuation context by calculating separate values in a first step and aggregating them to a total value (Burger & Ulbrich 2005, p. 531).[19] While value additivity is accepted in theory, it is examined by researchers whether company groups are traded at a discount compared to the individual subsidiary values – with ambiguous results (Koller, Goedhart & Wessels 2005). In this thesis, a possible 'conglomerate discount' is irrelevant as a theoretical DCF view is adopted in contrast to a market value view.

(2) Subsidiary controlling and PMS

PMS are a central instrument of subsidiary controlling. The use of PMS is not restricted to the context of controlling subsidiaries though. Therefore, literature on the topic is not tailored to the specific needs of subsidiary controlling. In this thesis it is attempted to bridge this gap.

---

[19] An important precondition to value additivity is the possibility to unambiguously assign components of the valuation (especially CFs) to the respective objects of valuation (Burger & Ulbrich 2005, p. 532). This is a common problem in different valuation contexts, cp. for instance Schlegel (2008, pp. 7-8) for the valuation of intangible assets.

(3) <u>VBM and PMS</u>

On the one hand, PMS concepts are influenced by VBM as increasing CV is introduced as the top organisational goal and value-based performance measures are introduced. On the other hand, VBM heavily depends on PMS to operationalise and enforce the concept of value-based management. The success of VBM depends on how well targets can be broken on performance measures (cp. chapter 4.2.2).

(4) <u>The topic as an interface of subsidiary controlling, VBM and PMS</u>

The topic of this thesis is located at the interface of the three disciplines. It is intended to provide an integrated view of how a value-based management of subsidiaries can be implemented with the help of PMS.

3 Financial performance measures

3.1 Introduction

3.1.1 Criteria for the evaluation of financial measures

The following criteria for the evaluation and comparison of performance measures have been compiled from several authors (Merchant & Van der Stede 2007, pp. 32-35; Schumann 2008, pp. 102-105; Schultze & Hirsch 2004, p. 32; Weber et al. 2004, pp. 85-86) and classified into categories.

(1) Control-relevance (behaviour control function)
In order that employees are motivated to perform activities which increase company value, two relations are crucial: First, the individual measures used to evaluate employees must be connected to the corporate objectives *(congruence)*. In the context of VBM, a measure's congruence depends on its ability to track SV development, i.e. it must be correlated highly with changes in SV (Merchant & Van der Stede 2007, p. 437). Second, the respective employees must be able to materially influence the outcome *(controllability)*. On the other hand, the person who is being evaluated should not be able to manipulate the measure and it should not be biased *(objectivity)*.

(2) Decision-relevance (information function)
Precision refers to randomness in the measurement, i.e. the variance of a series of independent measurements should approach zero. Moreover, the time lag between the performance and the possibility to measure it should be as small as possible *(timeliness)*. This is important because in case there are any problems they can be recognised timely and interventions are possible. Furthermore, the measure is supposed to not only show deviations between an actual and a target value, but also provide a possibility to examine the causes *(analysability)*. Additionally, *consideration of risk* is a criterion.

(3) Practical considerations

In order for the control and the motivation to be effective, employees must understand the measures and especially know how they can influence the result *(understandability)*. Furthermore, the necessary information and infrastructure to calculate the measure must be available *(feasibility)*. However, the benefit from the calculation of the measures should be greater than the cost of implementation and periodical calculation (*cost efficiency)*.

(4) Suitability for subsidiary management

This category is introduced in addition to the general criteria that can be found in literature in order to ensure that the subsequent analysis is tailored to the objectives of this thesis. In particular, *comparability* between subsidiaries is crucial and and *aggregation* of measures should be possible.[20]

As *precision* is more a problem when it comes to measuring 'soft' performance aspects such as social responsibility, this criterion is not used in the following. Furthermore, the *practical criteria (3)* are not considered either since they are no inherent problems of the measures but rather difficulties in their application. Additionally, it is very questionable how the costs and especially benefits of the use of individual measures should be quantified.

3.1.2 Classification possibilities and measure categories

3.1.2.1 Accounting, cash flow and capital market measures

While in Germany there has traditionally been a strong separation of *financial* accounting and *management* **accounting**, recently a convergence of the two areas can be observed. The importance of financial accounting for internal control purposes is increasing (Borchers 2000, p. 167; Krupp

---

[20] The possibility of aggregation is important if data is supposed to be analysed in multiple dimensions or layers, for instance by using Online Analytical Processing (OLAP) software tools.

2007, p. 72). The main reasons are the aspiration for leaner structures as company groups grow more complex (Borchers 2000, p. 167) and the introduction of International Financial Reporting Standards (IFRS). On the one hand, IFRS lead to a shift towards internal data. One example is segment reporting according to IFRS 8 where segments are identified according to the so-called management approach, i.e. according to internal reporting structures (Hoffjan 2009, p. 205; Borchers 2000, p. 168).[21] On the other hand, the more realistic representation of the economic situation in comparison to HGB regulations increase the external reports' utility for internal purposes (Hoffjan 2009, p. 203). Therefore, no distinction will be made between managerial and financial accounting measures in the following.

While accounting profit is a fictitious measure, **CF** is observable. CF often occurs asynchronously to its causation while accounting intends to report a correct profit of the period by using accruals (Ewert & Wagenhofer 2008, p. 525; Brignall 2007, p. 16).

Capital market measures are derived from share prices. Stock-based compensation plans are commonly used in practice, especially in the U.S. (Küpper 2008, p. 286; Merchant & Van der Stede 2007, p. 437).

3.1.2.2 Traditional and values-based measures

Traditional measures do not take into account the cost of equity (Faul 2004, p. 177). It is not deducted as an expense in accounting measures and does not lead to an outgoing payment either.

Value-based measures are based on the idea that value is only created if the income earned is higher than the cost of capital. Thus, a business that

---

[21] Another example is the percentage-of-completion method for construction contracts in which "contract revenues and contract costs (…) should be recognised (…) respectively by reference to the stage of completion of the contract" (IAS 11.22). This requires an elaborate internal project controlling.

breaks even in terms of accounting profits is actually making a loss. The idea of treating required return on equity as a cost was already promoted by Anthony (1973) and other scholars[22] long before the concept of the residual income was refined by Stern-Stewart with their EVA (Brealey, Myers & Allen 2008, p. 335; Stern, Stewart & Chew 1996, p. 224). There are also value-based measures which are derived from CF instead of accounting figures, e.g. CFROI.

Many value-based measures have been developed by consulting firms who market them aggressively (Garvey & Milbourn 2000, p. 210). Thus a critical reflection of the measures and publications is indispensable – especially concerning empirical studies by researchers affiliated with the firms who claim to prove a superiority of the respective measure.[23]

3.1.2.3 Relative and absolute measures

Absolute measures are single numbers, sums, differences or averages. Relative measures (ratios) relate different figures to each other (Meyer 2007, p. 22; Preißler 2008, p. 13).

In the context of financial performance measurement, absolute measures are in particular profit, CF and other types of income. Relative measures are especially return measures.

3.1.2.4 Concluding categorisation of financial measures

In the following chapter, the measures shown in Figure 5 will be presented. The discussion is not meant to be comprehensive in terms of the measures discussed. Instead, the measures presented are representatives of categories of measures which share similar characteristics and thus advantages and disadvantages.

---

[22] Küting & Eidel (1999, p. 832) even name a source from 1912.

[23] Cp. for instance O'Byrne (1997) with his article 'EVA® and Shareholder Return' which was published at a time when he was Senior Vice President at Stern Stewart & Company.

	Traditional	Value-based
Accounting-based	Profit **ROI** etc.	EVA / MVA
Cash flow-based	CF **CF return**	**CFROI** / CVA
Capital mar-ket-based	Share price / **Return** **SR, TR, jα, dr**	

bold = relative

Figure 5: Classification of financial performance measures
Source: Own illustration

First, *traditional* accounting and CF measures will be discussed. Next, *value-based* accounting and CF measures will be addressed. Finally, *capital marketmeasures* – which can neither be clearly categorised as traditional nor as value-based – will be dealt with.

3.2 Discussion and evaluation of measure categories

3.2.1 Traditional measures

3.2.1.1 Examples

There is a variety of *profit measures* which differ for instance in the consideration of taxes, interest, extraordinary positions and non-operating positions. There is also a number of *accounting return measures* – e.g. Return on Investment (ROI), Return on Net Assets (RONA) or Return on Capital Employed (ROCE) – which vary in the type of profit and capital measure used and are all designed according to the same principle:

$$Return = \frac{Profit}{Capital}$$

CF measures can be calculated based on a variety of fund definitions and also differ depending on the accounting regulations applied (Britzelmaier

2009, pp. 39-61). They can also be referred to invested capital in order to calculate *CF return* (Preißler 2008, pp. 70-71).

3.2.1.2 Evaluation

Goal congruence: First of all *profit and CF* are past-oriented single period measures, i.e. they do not indicate value which is determined by future payments. Moreover, they do not take into account many changes which create firm value, for instance when a firm is granted a patent (Merchant & Van der Stede 2007, p. 442). Furthermore, even if they are forecasted and discounted, *profit measures* show systematic deviations resulting from accruals as Küpper (2008, p. 271) formally shows by means of depreciation: From a DCF standpoint, the purchase price (P_0) is immediately recognised at t=0 whereas in accounting is it depreciated (P_0/n) and by discounting presented too small (i.e. the PV is too big) which can lead to overinvestment:

$$\sum_{t=1}^{n} \frac{CF - \frac{P_0}{n}}{(1+i)^t} = \sum_{t=1}^{n} \frac{CF}{(1+i)^t} - \sum_{t=1}^{n} \frac{\frac{P_0}{n}}{(1+i)^t} \quad > \quad \sum_{t=1}^{n} \frac{CF_t}{(1+i)^t} - P_0$$

PV of profits   **PV of CFs**

Moreover, profit is often conservatively biased. However, this strongly depends on the accounting principles applied. It is for instance often assumed that IFRS profit tracks value better than HGB profit. Additional reasons for deviations are the fact that profit ignores the cost of investments in working capital, the cost of equity and the time value of money (Faul 2004, pp. 177-180; Britzelmaier 2009, p. 19).

For *CF*, the accrual problem does not occur. If CF is defined consistently with the DCF method, the PV is congruent (since this factually *is* the DCF method). However, the criticism concerning past-orientation of single-period measures and not reflecting certain changes in value is still applicable. Moreover, due to their asynchronous occurrence with their causation and their greater variance, they are not a very good indicator of actual performance (Ewert & Wagenhofer 2008, p. 532)

Traditional measures are usually largely **controllable** by managers as they can be tailored to the authority limits of the respective manager. For instance, a manager could be made responsible only for certain items from the income statement or for the income of certain products (Merchant & Van der Stede 2007, p. 441).

While *accounting profit* can be influenced by accounting policy, *CF* is a more **objective** measure since it can hardly be manipulated (Küpper 2008, p. 273; Faul 2004, pp. 181-182). However, if CF is determined by the indirect method, it is based on profit so that the same problems occur (Schumann 2008)[24]. On the other hand, financial statements are verified by auditing firms and corporate policies can be specified to be used in all divisions so that they are more objective and comparable within the group.

Timeliness of traditional measures is limited. First, depending on the length of the measurement period, results are only reported with a time lag. Second, the effects of certain decisions are only measurable with delay. For instance investments in intangible assets might only lead to income after some time (Weber et al. 2004, p. 96)

A well-known measure system to further analyse *ROI* is the DuPont system (Meyer 2007, pp. 139-144). However, the **analysability** is confined to the financial composition of the result. As pointed out in chapter 2.2.4, financial measures only show results of entrepreneurial activity, not causes so that analysability remains limited.

Traditional measures ignore **risk**. However, from an investor's point of view, risk is crucial. For more risky investments, a risk premium is required.

For *return measures* the respective points of criticism of profit and CF are also valid as they appear in the numerator. Moreover, return measures

---

[24] This is only true to a limited extent since in the indirect calculation of CF important positions for accounting policy (depreciation and provisions) are eliminated.

have the tendency to induce sub-optimisation and can include a systematic age bias if they use book values in the denominator (see chapter 3.3).

In terms of **comparability**, the absolute measures *profit* and *CF* are biased by size, i.e. bigger subsidiaries have higher profits ceteris paribus. *Return measures* can be directly compared.

Aggregation of *profits* and *CF* can be easily done by adding them up. Traditional *return measures* have to be weighted by the invested capital, which should be easily possible as the capital figure is already needed in the calculation of the return measure.

3.2.2 Value-based measures

3.2.2.1 Examples

Economic Value Added (EVA) is discussed as a representative of residual income measures. They are based on the above-mentioned idea that the cost of capital has to be deducted from profit. EVA is calculated as follows (Horváth 2006, p. 490):[25]

$$EVA = NOPAT - WACC * NA$$

The WACC is calculated based on the CAPM as shown in chapter 2.3.2. Both Net Operating Profit After Tax (NOPAT) – which is a profit after taxes before interest[26] – and Net Assets (NA) are derived from the financial statements (Stern, Stewart & Chew 1996, p. 224; Horváth 2006, p. 490). The distinctiveness of EVA are the conversions of NOPAT and NA which are performed in order to convert the figures from the perspective of creditor protection (accounting model) to a market and shareholder-oriented view (economic model) (Schumann 2008, p. 121; Britzelmaier 2009, p.

---

[25] The formula displayed is the *capital charge method*. It can mathematically be converted into the *value spread method* (Britzelmaier 2009, pp. 117-118; Schumann 2008, p. 121):
*NOPAT – WACC * NA* → *RONA * NA – WACC * NA* → *(RONA – WACC) * NA*

[26] = EBIT – tax. The interest is not deducted as it is taken into account by deducting the COC from NOPAT.

120). The extent of the conversions largely depends on the accounting regulation which the numbers are based on (Britzelmaier 2009, p. 122). In comparison to HGB, the use of IFRS figures requires less conversion, especially if necessary conversions are anticipated in the preparation of the IFRS statement (Hoffjan 2009, p. 218). [27]

While EVA itself can be used for past-oriented performance measurement, forecasted EVA figures can be discounted in order to get the *Market Value Added (MVA)*. By adding the MVA – which is today's value of future excess profits – to the NA, the company's value is calculated as shown in Figure 6 (Schumann 2008, p. 123).

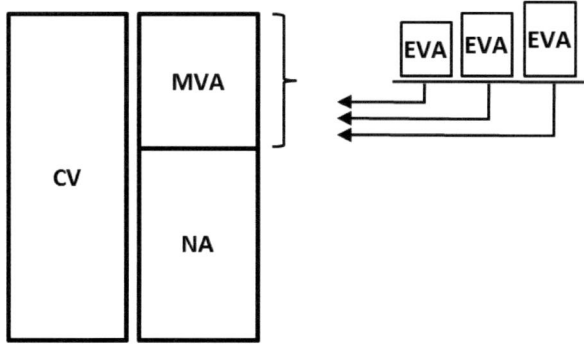

Figure 6: Relationship between EVA, MVA and CV
Source: Mittendorfer (Value Based Management in der Unternehmenspraxis 2004, p. 101)

A relative value-based measure is *Cash Flow Return on Investment (CFROI)*. It is based on CF and inflation-adjusted. Mathematically, it is calculated with the help of the internal rate of return (IRR) method based on single-period figures which are derived from the financial statement: Gross

---

[27] For instance the correction of degressive depreciation and the recognition of finance leases are already part of IFRS (Trützschler, Tomaszweski & Blome 2007, p. 403)

cash investment (GCI), Gross cash flow (GCF), asset life and terminal value (Langguth 2008, p. 166).[28]

It is important to realise that although the use of IRR implies a dynamic view, CFROI is actually a static measure since it is based on historical single-period data instead of projected data (Young & O'Byrne 2001, pp. 383-384). The modified version introduced in 1998 ($CFROI_{mod}$) renounces on IRR and calculates the return based on the following formula (Britzelmaier 2009, p. 156):

$$CFROI_{mod} = \frac{GCF - Economic\ Depreciation}{GCI}$$

Economic depreciation is an annuity which distributes the GCI over the asset life so that at the end of the asset life the GCI is earned back. It takes into account compounded interest effects so that the depreciation is less than a traditional straight-line depreciation. CFROI and $CFROI_{mod}$ do not lead to the same result (Britzelmaier 2009, pp. 156-159).

By comparing CFROI to WACC and multiplying the difference by the GCI, the *Cash Value Added (CVA)* is calculated. It is an absolute measure of value creation, i.e. a residual income measure like EVA. The main difference to EVA is that the invested assets are gross (cp. also chapter 3.3.1).

3.2.2.2 Evaluation

Goal congruence: Both *EVA* and *CFROI* are past-oriented, single-period measures. Thus there is only a link to SV if the measures are examined over the whole life of an investment, but not for a single period (Langguth 2008, p. 183; Schultze & Hirsch 2004, p. 65).

---

[28] For a detailed explanation of calculation and adjustments cp. for instance Britzelmaier (Kompakt-Training Wertorientierte Unternehmensführung 2009, pp. 146-163) or Langguth (Kapitalmarktorientiertes Wertmanagement 2008, pp. 166-173).

So, MVA might be congruent with SV. In order that goal congruence of MVA can be confirmed, the PV of future EVA figures must equal the company value at any time (Schumann 2008, p. 108). This is true if the following equation holds (Schumann 2008, p. 124; Küpper 2008, p. 281)[29]:

$$CV_{DCF} = NA + MVA$$

$$\sum_{t=1}^{n} \frac{FCF_t}{(1 + WACC_t)^t} = NA + \sum_{t=1}^{n} \frac{EVA_t}{(1 + WACC_t)^t}$$

According to the Preinreich-Lücke theorem[30], the PV of cash flows and the PV of residual income figure are identical under certain conditions (Kruschwitz 2007, p. 199; Küpper 2008, pp. 168-172) which means that the equation could hold. However, in case of EVA the theorem is only applicable under tight assumptions (Weber et al. 2004, p. 89; Küpper 2008, pp. 275-276).[31]

Another problem regarding the goal congruence of EVA and CVA is the fact that the capital charge is based on (modified) book values which does not correspond to market value capital from the investors' perspective. Thus, part of the actually supplied capital is not compensated for (Weber et al. 2004, pp. 89, 95). Therefore, *Refined Economic Value Added (REVA)* multiplies the WACC with the capital's market value instead of NA (Young & O'Byrne 2001, p. 260). Küting and Eidel (1999, pp. 834-835) argue that REVA is not correct from a theoretical standpoint since it combines two incompatible components: profit based on book values and market values

---

[29] Weber et al (Wertorientierte Unternehmenssteuerung 2004, p. 148) use the formula $SV^{DCF} = NA + MVA - FK^{DCF}$ which is equivalent to the displayed equation since SV + FK = CV.

[30] In Anglophone literature, this effect is discussed under the headline 'clean surplus accounting' (Ewert & Wagenhofer 2008, p. 537).

[31] Küpper (Controlling. Konzeption, Aufgaben, Instrumente. 2008, p. 276) points out that if the premises of Preinreich-Lücke theorem were applicable in practice, a simple correction of HGB profit would track value which means that the conversions of EVA were not necessary and more simple residual income measures could be used which require only minor changes of accounting systems.

of capital. However, it has to be noted that EVA also in its original version is already inconsistent: First, EVA compares actual *book* returns (RONA) with required *market* returns (WACC) (Langguth 2008, p. 152). Second, the capital structure used in WACC (target capital structure) is inconsistent with the capital base that it is multiplied by in the calculation of EVA (Weber et al. 2004, p. 91).

An issue concerning CFROI is that the IRR method assumes a reinvestment of gains at the IRR. In contrast, CFROI$_{mod}$ assumes that interest is compounded with the COC (Weber et al. 2004, p. 93). Which assumption is more realistic depends on the individual business.

Küting & Eidel (1999, pp. 835-836) make up situations in which an increase of EVA actually results in a *de*crease of CV as opposed to Stewart's claim that a rising EVA leads to a rising company value. Also for CFROI it is true that from a positive measure it cannot be concluded that there has been an increase in value (Schumann 2008, p. 148).

Despite the harsh criticism from a theoretical point of view, the measures are useful in practice as they *do* motivate managers to engage in activities that are consistent with value creation, i.e. to take investments that offer a return higher than the COC (Anthony & Govindarajan 2001, p. 260).

Controllability of value-based measures is more difficult than for accounting measures since it is not possible to confine responsibility to certain income statement positions. Additionally, employees who are evaluated by value-based measures should have competences for resource allocation since invested capital forms part of the measure (Young & O'Byrne 2001, p. 431; Weber et al. 2004, p. 97). Although resource allocation is usually determined by the corporate centre, probably most subsidiary managers can decide over individual investments so that they can reject value-destroying investments and take value-adding investments.

As *EVA* is based on accounting data, **objectivity** is comparable to accounting measures. Conversions neutralise some of the accounting policy. However, conversions offer new options and scope of discretion (Schultze & Hirsch 2004, p. 73; Langguth 2008, p. 182). *CFROI* components are largely independent from accounting policy. For instance depreciations do not affect it since a gross capital base is used (Schultze & Hirsch 2004, p. 79; Langguth 2008, pp. 183-184).

In terms of **timeliness**, the same argumentation as for accounting measures is applicable.

Value-based measures can be **analysed** in terms of their composition by their elements which enter into the formula comparably to the DuPont system for ROI. Additionally, value drivers can be determined which also show qualitative influence factors on EVA. However, they are more useful for ex ante value management since it is hard to quantitatively analyse the influences with hindsight.

Value-based measures do consider **risk** as the COC which is deducted from profit depends on beta (systematic risk). However, it is discussable if only systematic risk should be taken into account (cp. chapter 3.2.3.2).

In terms of **comparability** it is often criticised that EVA is an absolute measures and thus not comparable since it is biased by size which means that big subsidiaries earn a higher EVA than small ones ceteris paribus. In contrast, CFROI is a relative measure and thus comparable (Young & O'Byrne 2001, p. 415; Erasmus & Lambrechts 2006, p. 16). On the other hand, EVA proponents argue that this criticism is based on confusion about measurement objectives and that the value creation is supposed to be measured in a currency amount (Young & O'Byrne 2001, p. 416). The discussed size effect is shown in Figure 7. It can be seen that in the right chart EVA is higher although return is lower due to the higher investment amount.

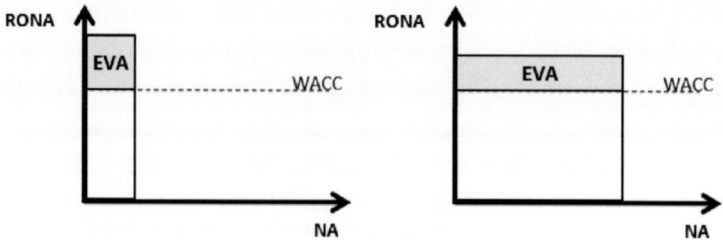

Figure 7: Value creation and investment amount
Source: With adaptations from Burger & Ulbrich (2005, p. 567)

Concerning **aggregation**, Ewert und Wagenhofer (2000, pp. 54-55) formally show that the sum of subsidiary EVA is regularly <u>not</u> equal to the corporate EVA when calculated separately. The reason is the above-explained inconsistency in the calculation of COC since WACC calculation is based on market values and multiplied with NA (book values). Therefore, EVA can only be aggregated by adding up if the following is true for every subsidiary i:

$$\frac{NA_i}{total\ NA} = \frac{market\ value_i}{total\ market\ value}$$

As in REVA, market value of capital is used instead of NA it can be aggregated by simple addition.[32] As this reasoning is rather complex and not quite intuitive, an exemplary calculation can be found in Appendix 1.

3.2.3 Capital market measures

3.2.3.1 <u>Examples and transfer to industrial companies</u>

Capital market measures are based on a company's share price or return on the share, i.e. percentage changes of the price in a given period. Returns can be calculated discretely (assuming reinvestment only at the end

---

[32] Therefore, it could be argued that REVA is calculated more consistently than EVA in contrary to what critics of REVA claim (cp. above).

of the period) or continuously (assuming reinvestment in infinitesimally small periods) which is the common method in finance.[33]

More elaborate measures are used in the financial industry for the evaluation of portfolios' and fund managers' performance. Subsequently, these concepts will be discussed and transferred to industrial companies.

In the context of financial investment analysis, *performance* is defined as a *risk-adjusted* return relative to a *benchmark return*, i.e. the models intend to show a systematic relation between risk and expected returns (Fischer 2001, p. 271). A typical structure of measures looks as follows (Steiner & Bruns 2002, pp. 595-597):

$$Performance = \left(\frac{Return - Benchmark\ return}{Risk\ measure}\right)$$

A classically used measure is the **Sharpe ratio (SR)** which relates the excess return in comparison to the risk free rate (government bonds) to the standard deviation of returns of a portfolio (Fischer 2001, p. 271). It can be interpreted as excess return per unit of total (systematic and unsystematic) risk.

$$SR = \left(\frac{R - r_f}{\sigma}\right)$$

---

[33] The main advantage of using continuous returns is that they can easily be operated with, e.g. they can be extended into multiple periods by simply adding them up (Jorion 2001, pp. 99-101). In order to ensure consistency, if several returns are used in one measure (for instance if actual returns are compared to expected returns according to the CAPM) they must all be based on the same calculation method. Furthermore, a correct consideration of dividends is important which is done as follows:

$$R_t = \ln\left(\frac{P_{t,ex-dividend}+D_t}{P_{t-1,ex-dividend}}\right) = \ln\left(\frac{P_{t,cum-dividend}}{P_{t-1,ex-dividend}}\right)$$

The **Treynor ratio (TR)** is calculated as the Sharpe ratio but uses the portfolio's beta instead of its standard deviation as a risk measure (Fischer 2001, p. 274). Thus, it measures excess return per unit of systematic risk.

$$TR = \left(\frac{R - r_f}{\beta}\right)$$

Jensen's alpha (jα) is an absolute measure which compares the actual return to the expected return according to the CAPM. In fund management, it is interpreted as the ability of a fund manager to spot undervalued stocks (Fischer 2001, p. 275). It could also be interpreted as the finance discipline's equivalent to residual income (expressed as percentage return).

$$j\alpha = R - \mu = R - [r_f + \beta * (r_m - r_f)]$$

Differential return (dr) is the equivalent to Jensen's alpha using the investment's total risk compared to the market portfolio's total risk as a risk measure:

$$j\alpha = R - \mu = R - [r_f + \frac{\sigma}{\sigma_{market}}(r_{market} - r_f)]$$

The four presented classical measures can be classified into categories as shown in Figure 8. The absolute measures show excess return (in percent), but do not relate it back to risk, so that different investments cannot be compared (Fischer 2001, p. 276). Using an example, an excess return of 1 percent over a high required return of a risky investment is less than an excess return of 1 percent over a very safe investment. Therefore, absolute measures are excluded from the subsequent discussion.

	Total risk (σ)	Systematic risk (β)
Relative	Sharpe ratio (SR)	Treynor ratio (TR)
Absolute	Differential return (dr)	Jensen's alpha (jα)

Figure 8: Classification of capital market-based performance measures
Source: With adaptations from Fischer (Performanceanalyse in der Praxis 2001, p. 280)

The relative measures only differ in the risk measure they use. For a diversified investor, beta and thus Treynor ratio is the correct risk measure. Volatility or standard deviation of returns is a measure for total risk and thus correct for an investor who only invests in one portfolio (Eling & Schuhmacher 2007, p. 2633; Fischer 2001, p. 273). Thus, the author of this thesis suggests Sharpe ratio as the most appropriate measure for the purpose of the evaluation of an industrial company's management's performance. From an individual shareholder's point of view, a perfect diversification cannot be assumed. This notion is in line with Ballwieser (2007, pp. 94-95) who argues that neglecting unsystematic risk is inadequate when valuing a company that is not part of a portfolio.[34] Also other renowned academics as cited by Petersen, Plenborg, & Schøler (2006, p. 43) argue that in the valuation of privately held firms, non-systematic risk should be taken into account.

A common criticism against volatility as a risk measure is that it is only appropriate for normally distributed return while in reality normal distributions do not describe share price movements very well (Brailsford, Heaney &

---

[34] This is also a criticism against using CAPM for other purposes such as determining discount rates in company valuation or COC rates in value-based measures as this way only systematic risk is accounted for.

Bilson 2006, p. 271; Steiner & Bruns 2002, p. 601). Therefore, new performance measures use different types of risk measures, e.g. drawdown or Value at Risk (VAR). [35] However, despite the incorrect assumption of normally distributed returns, several recent studies report that the comparison of investments by means of the new measures leads to the same ranking as an evaluation by Sharpe ratio (Eling & Schuhmacher 2007, pp. 2633-2636). Thus, Sharpe ratio can be considered appropriate.

For the purpose of management evaluation in an industrial company, as a **benchmark return** the return on the market portfolio or on a portfolio of the peer group's shares (e.g. weighted by market capitalisation or arithmetic mean) can be imagined in order to eliminate distortions by cyclical stock market trends. Peer group benchmarks have the advantage that they eliminate cyclical trends in both the overall stock market and the industry. The ratio following from this argumentation will be called Adjusted Sharpe Ratio (ASR) subsequently:

$$ASR = \frac{(R_{Company} - R_{PG})}{\sigma_{Company}}$$

It has to be emphasised though that the measure is very tight as it is only positive if the stocks *outperforms* the competitors' stocks as opposed to the original Sharpe ratio where only the risk free rate has to be beaten.

3.2.3.2 Evaluation

In terms of **congruence**, since the goal of value-based management (cp. chapter 2.3.1) was defined as maximising DCF value and not market value, capital market-oriented measures are not completely congruent. However, it was also said that they provide a close proxy to the theoretical value. Also, they are future-oriented so that a certain level of congruence is given. Benchmark measures such as the ASR presented above do <u>not</u> measure

---

[35] For an overview on risk measures cp. Steiner & Bruns (Wertpapiermanagement. Professionelle Wertpapieranalyse und Portfoliostrukturierung. 2002, p. 601).

value creation. If the whole industry performs below COC, the measure does not signal this.

Share price is only **controllable** partly by top management. The influence of lower-level employees or subsidiary managers is too small to base their remuneration on market prices of the company group. Even for top managers, the market price includes many uncontrollable factors such as the general macroeconomic situation. Therefore it makes sense to use relative performance by including an industry benchmark return (as shown above) and thus neutralise macroeconomic and industry cycles (Küpper 2008, p. 289; Merchant & Van der Stede 2007, pp. 437-439).

Capital market-oriented measures can generally be seen as **objective** as manipulation of the stock market is difficult and monitored by authorities and exchanges. Küpper (2008, p. 289) mentions the importance that measures are able to record correctly transaction with shareholders such as dividends or changes in capital in order to avoid manipulation.

Merchant & Van der Stede (2007, p. 437) claim that market measures are **timely** as market values are available on a daily or even more frequent basis. It has to be pointed out though, that the mere availability of data does not mean that the measurement of actual changes in value is timely. In this thesis it is argued that market prices are a delayed indicator of value creation depending on when internal information becomes public.

Analysability of reasons concerning the development of capital-market measures is limited to capital market data. Internal value drivers cannot be derived.

Concerning the **consideration of risk**, relative market measures such as the SR are better than using plain share price or return as they explicitly take into account risk. In contrast to value-based measures, SR also takes into account unsystematic risk which is more adequate in a non-diversified context.

Suitability for subsidiary controlling in general is limited since the measures are only available for listed companies and it is assumed that most subsidiaries are not listed. However, in order to track the performance of individual business units, some companies have issued so-called *tracking stocks*. They are traded as common stocks in addition to the regular corporate stocks. Shareholders receive a dividend based on the performance of the sub-unit. However, the use of tracking stocks is not very common, also because of the high costs related to issuing stocks and being listed (Jalbert & Landry 2003, pp. 33-34).

Concerning **comparability**, SR is a very good measure since the return is risk-adjusted and thus comparable even if subsidiaries are exposed to a different risk.

Simple returns can be **aggregated** by weighting them with the subsidiary's (market) values. SR, however, cannot be easily aggregated because standard deviation is included. The standard deviation of a company group's portfolio of subsidiaries is regularly not a simple weighted average. Instead, risk diversification effects have to be taken into account by including correlations between returns (Perridon & Steiner 2007, pp. 242-243).

3.3 Dysfunctions and biases of financial measures

3.3.1 Age bias

3.3.1.1 Problem

Age bias is a bias that is originated in accounting depreciation. Depreciation is usually 'front-end loaded' (straight-line or declining depreciation) while 'back-end loaded' depreciation schedules which would alleviate the problem are not permitted according to most regulations (Holler 2009, p. 76).

Depreciation leads to a decreasing net book value if no further investments are made which has the following effects on financial measures: In
accounting return measures – for instance ROI – the denominator decreases over the life cycle of an investment, i.e. ROI automatically increases if profit is constant (Merchant & Van der Stede 2007, p. 449). In
residual income measures – for instance EVA – the capital charge is relatively high in the first years and low in the last years due to decreasing NA
although NOPAT and WACC stay constant, i.e. ceteris paribus EVA automatically increases over the investment's life (Weber et al. 2004, p. 90;
Holler 2009, p. 76).

These effects also have implications for the behaviour of managers: They
are a disincentive for investment. Managers will refrain from investing although the PV of future income is sufficiently large – especially if they ex-
pect to leave the company since assets at the beginning of their useful life
tend to deteriorate the measures (Jensen & Meckling 2009, p. 54; Holler
2009, p. 76). Moreover, there is an incentive to privilege short-term investments, i.e. investments with a fast depreciation, while longer-term investments, for example in research and development (R&D) are refrained
from. Additionally, resources might be allocated to divisions with older assets since they seem to be relatively more profitable. Furthermore, assets
are retained beyond their optimal life (Merchant & Van der Stede 2007, p.
450).

Weber et al (2006, p. 90) argue that the effect of a decreasing book value
is hardly relevant in practice since they assume the assets' age structure
to be constant, i.e. that the average asset's age is constant as assets are
replaced regularly. In contrast, Brealey & Myers (2008, pp. 341-342) show
that errors only offset in the long run if the company is not growing. The
extent of the error depends on how fast the company is growing.

3.3.1.2 Possible solutions

As pointed out above, the cause of age bias is accounting depreciation. Therefore, there are two possible types of solutions which are both related to depreciation.

First, *gross investment* – i.e. an undepreciated capital base – or replacement values can be used as a reference in the calculation of ROI and EVA (Merchant & Van der Stede 2007, p. 450). This way, the capital base which is charged remains constant. While CFROI uses a gross investment base, this can also easily be done to adjust regular accounting measures or EVA.

Second, the depreciation schedule can be changed. For instance, *economic depreciation* can be used. Please note, that this is *not* economic depreciation in the sense of CFROI, but economic depreciation as explained by Brealey & Myers (2008, pp. 340-341): Economic depreciation is the reduction in PV of future CFs from one period to the subsequent one.[36] By deducting it from CF, economic income is measured.

$$Economic\ Income = CF_1 + (PV_1 - PV_0)$$

By referring economic income to the PV, the economic rate of return is calculated.

$$Economic\ return = \frac{Economic\ income}{PV_0} = \frac{CF_1 + (PV_1 - PV_0)}{PV_0}$$

Another way to adapt the depreciation schedule is to use *sinking-fund depreciation* as suggested by authors associated with Stern Stewart & Co

---

[36] PV changes as time moves forward for two reasons: On the one hand, CFs of past periods are not part of the stream anymore (PV decreases). On the other hand, future CFs 'move closer', i.e. their discounted value is increasing (PV increases). For constant CF streams, the first phenomenon outweighs the second, so that PV decreases (economic depreciation). In the special case where CF is equal to the 'old' PV multiplied by the discount rate, PV does not change.

(Young & O'Byrne 2001, p. 416). Thereby, the initial investment is distributed over the useful life using the annuity factor[37]. The composition of the
annuity changes over the useful life – in the beginning the interest part is
bigger while in the end the depreciation part dominates (Schultze & Hirsch
2004, pp. 71-72).

In Figure 9 a simplified calculation of different measures for a constant CF
stream can be seen. The COC used in the measures was chosen equal to
the IRR of the stream so that the created value should equal zero.

	Period		1	2	3	4	5	6
	CF	-1000	250	250	250	250	250	250
Accounting / EVA	NA beginning		1000	833	667	500	333	167
	Depreciation (straight-line)		-167	-167	-167	-167	-167	-167
	Profit (CF - Depr.)		83	83	83	83	83	83
	Return		8%	10%	13%	17%	25%	50%
	Residual Income (EVA)		-46	-25	-3	18	40	62
	Discounted EVA (Σ=MVA)		-41	-19	-2	11	22	30
CFROI mod.	Gross Inv		1000	1000	1000	1000	1000	1000
	Ec. Depr.		-120	-120	-120	-120	-120	-120
	CF - Ec. Depr.		130	130	130	130	130	130
	CFROI		13%	13%	13%	13%	13%	13%
	Residual Income (CVA)		0	0	0	0	0	0
Economic depreciation	PV beginning		1000	880	744	591	417	221
	PV end		880	744	591	417	221	0
	Ec. Depr.		-120	-136	-153	-173	-196	-221
	Ec. Income (CF - Ec. Depr.)		130	114	97	77	54	29
	Ec. Return		13%	13%	13%	13%	13%	13%
	Residual Income		0	0	0	0	0	0
Sinking-fund depreciation	Capital base (beginning)		1000	880	744	591	417	221
	Annuity		-250	-250	-250	-250	-250	-250
	thereof capital charge		-130	-114	-97	-77	-54	-29
	thereof depreciation		-120	-136	-153	-173	-196	-221
	Profit		130	114	97	77	54	29
	Return		13%	13%	13%	13%	13%	13%
	Residual Income		0	0	0	0	0	0

Figure 9: Age bias of different performance measures
Source: Own calculations

The following conclusions can be drawn from the calculation:

---

[37] $Annuity\ factor = \frac{(1+i)^n * i}{(1+i)^n - 1}$

➢ With straight-line depreciation, the age bias can clearly be seen with an ROI ranging from 8 percent to 50 percent and EVA ranging from -46 to 62.

➢ Both of the discussed improvements – using gross investment or an adjusted depreciation schedule – relieve the age bias.

➢ A correct return and residual income can be measured with several depreciation schedules, i.e. different accruals of period income are possible. However, it has to be noticed that with different CF structures that are not constant, the results differ which is shown in Appendix 2.

It could be shown that age bias can be relieved by two types of adjustments. Among the changes of depreciation schedule, economic depreciation can be considered as conceptually superior in terms of goal congruence since it measures changes in DCF value directly. However, the question is how the conceptual superiority can be realised in practice since exact projections of CF are hardly possible. Furthermore it is harder to apply on an aggregated level than the other concepts. Therefore, in practice the use of CFROI or sinking-fund depreciation might be a better choice.

3.3.2 Short-termism

3.3.2.1 Problem

The term *short-termism* refers to decisions in which companies pursue a course of action that maximises short-term gains but is suboptimal for the long-term (Laverty 2004, p. 949). Short-termism can occur when there is an intertemporal trade-off, i.e. when optimal short-term results do *not* extrapolate into optimal long-term results (Marginson & McAulay 2008, p. 274).

Short-termism is closely related to the concept of *intertemporal choice*. This is a characteristic of decisions in which the costs and benefits are distributed over time differently (Laverty 1996, pp. 827-828) . Figure 10 shows the development of net return on two investment alternatives. Alternative A has a relatively smooth distribution over time while alternative

B is less equally distributed. By calculating the PV, it could be determined which alternative is optimal. However, the alternatives have different implications for the timing of profit or payments.

There has to be found a balance between the short-term and long-term needs. While the ability to compete in the long run and long-term value creation is crucial, short-term goals cannot be ignored either if the company wants to survive in the short-term (Marginson & McAulay 2008, p. 274).

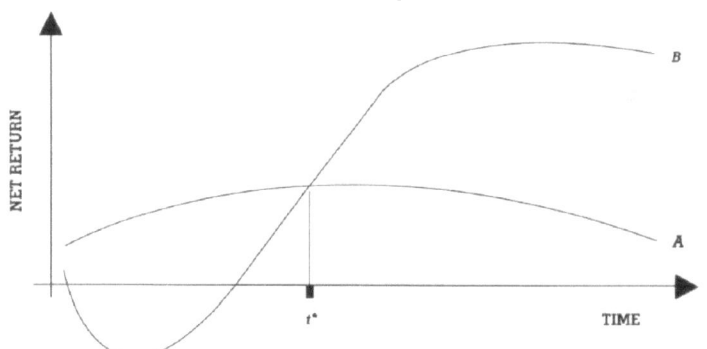

Figure 10: A problem of intertemporal choice
Source: Laverty (1996, p. 828)

In practice, there seems to be a preference for short-term performance (Marginson & McAulay 2008, p. 273). Merchant & Van der Stede (2007, pp. 443-444) distinguish between two types of short-termism: *Investment myopia* means that managers refrain from investments because they lead to low short-term performance even if they have a positive NPV. This is especially bad if the investments are important for long-term competitiveness, such as investments in research & development. *Operating myopia* means boosting profits of the current period at the expense of future periods and goodwill that has been created over a long time. This can for instance been done by decreasing quality, forcing employees to work harder or so-called channel stuffing, i.e. boosting near-term sales by lowering prices to the disadvantage of later sales.

Financial performance measures are often blamed to encourage short-termism (Neely, Gregory & Platts 1995, p. 106; Langfield-Smith, Thorne & Hilton 2009, p. 692). On the one hand, they make short-term performance visible. On the other hand, there are biases in accounting measures that favour short-termism, especially if the measures are derived from financial accounting (Marginson & McAulay 2008, p. 276; Merchant & Van der Stede 2007, pp. 443-444): As discussed in chapter 3.3.1, age bias can be a disincentive for investment. Furthermore, accounting measures are con-servatively biased. By often recognising costs earlier than revenues, there is a systematic understatement of profits. For instance projects with uncer-tain returns – such as investments in intangible assets or new product de-velopment– are often expensed as the costs are incurred although they are investments from an economic point of view. If classified as capital investment in accounting, they are usually depreciated over periods that are shorter than it takes to realise the revenues. With single-period CF-oriented measures, the problem is even worse because investments lead to immediate pay-outs and there is no accrual if incoming payments are delayed.

The above-mentioned biases lead to a negative impact of investments on short-term financial measures. That means that managers who intend to produce high short-term performance can do so by refraining from long-term investments.

3.3.2.2 Possible solutions

(1) Adjustment of individual measures

One way to adjust the measures is to measure SV directly by using *eco-nomic income* as explained in the context of age bias.

55

Another way is to improve accounting measures by *better matching reve-nues and expenses*. This can be done by making simple adjustments such as increasing depreciable lives or changing depreciation schedules. Fur-thermore, investments that were previously expensed directly should be capitalised and matched with later revenues[38] (Merchant & Van der Stede 2007, p. 481). The matching principle is already an integral part of the IFRS stating that expenses which are directly related to particular income should be recognised in the period in which the respective income is rec-ognised (F.95).[39]

Furthermore, a *disaggregation and reclassification of measures* could be thought of. For instance one could differentiate between revenues from old products and revenues from new products in order to motivate invest-ments in product development. Another way is to differentiate between operating expenses and developmental expenses. In such a concept, only short-term operating performance would be rewarded. The responsibility of developmental expenses is taken at a higher organisational level and managed with different controls. However, this approach has two main limitations: First, it is gameable since it is hard to distinguish between op-erating and developmental expenses. Second, the centralisation of devel-opmental responsibility has the disadvantage that higher level managers might not be as well informed as managers closer to business (Merchant & Van der Stede 2007, pp. 480-481).

---

[38] With BilMoG and IFRS there is already an improvement compared to old HGB figures since there is an obligation to capitalise development expenses according to IAS 38.57 and an option to do so according to the new version of §248 (2) HGB.

[39] A common application of the matching principle is the percentage-of-completion method according to IAS 11.22 (Weißenberger 2007, p. 60).

(2) Adjustment of other elements of the PMS[40]

Investment myopia can be addressed quite well with the above-explained adjustments. However, the general problem of short-termism has deeper causes such as stock market pressure or managerial opportunism. Some of the causes can be addressed as follows:

One suggestion is to *extend the measurement horizon*, i.e. extend the period which is used to measure and reward performance (Merchant & Van der Stede 2007, pp. 482-484). This has two advantages: First, it improves measurement since some measures are delayed and become more congruent with value-creation as the measurement period is extended. Second, by setting longer-term incentives, managers pay more attention to the long-term consequences of their decisions. However, as Merchant & Van der Stede (2007, p. 483) state, long-term incentives ought to be quite lucrative in order to achieve the desired motivational effects due to the uncertainty involved and the subjective preference for near-term payments which is a lot higher than the time value of money would suggest.

Accounting measures are past-oriented. Therefore, they should be *combined with future-oriented measures* so that there is a balance between long- and short-term incentives. The measures can be weighted differently to evaluate overall performance. As already indicated in chapter 2.2.4, non-financial measures can be used. Market share, product quality or customer satisfaction are good leading indicators of future financial performance. Also capital market measures are said to be future-oriented (within the limitations of capital market efficiency as discussed in this thesis) (Merchant & Van der Stede 2007, pp. 472-479). Laverty (2004, p. 959) suggests to use short-term measures only for feedback to project managers on their progress instead of evaluating them by the measures.

---

[40] Although chapter 3 is about financial performance measures, the following issues concerning PMS as an entity are discussed at this point because the problem of short-termism is generated by financial performance measures.

Another suggestion from literature is to *reduce short-term pressure*. As surveys show, managers especially feel pressured by short-term stock market expectations (Laverty 2004, p. 956). However, there has been a debate going on whether stock markets are really myopic or not (Marginson & McAulay 2008, p. 275). Empirical research often does not support this view.[41] A theoretical argument which supports the view that stock markets create short-term pressure is information asymmetry. As investors do not have complete information about future prospects, managers need to rely on short-term performance to prove their effort (Laverty 1996, p. 834). These concepts can be transferred to the inside of the company. There is also information asymmetry between different management levels. Marginson & McAulay (2008, p. 276) hypothesise that the perceived pressure is passed down from one hierarchical level to the next. Laverty (2004, p. 959) suggests top management to break this vicious circle by acting as a buffer in order to relieve middle managers from external pressures. This should be clearly communicated, e.g. by reducing the weight of quarterly profit targets. Furthermore, a corporate culture should be fostered which protects managers from having to make trade-offs between short-term and long-term and makes them feel that long-term achievements will be rewarded. However, it is also important to maintain some short-term pressure in order to prevent inefficient decisions-making, for instance building up unnecessary slack resources[42] and ensure motivation (Merchant & Van der Stede 2007, pp. 484, 34; Laverty 2004, pp. 950-951).

---

[41] For instance, significant positive returns can be found related to the announcement of R&D projects (Marginson & McAulay 2008, p. 275). Moreover, the high valuation of start-up companies with large short-term losses indicates a long-term focus of the capital market (Abarbanell & Bernard 2000). On the other hand, there are studies finding that stock markets do undervaluate future CFs in comparison to near-term CFs (Black & Fraser 2000, p. 152)

[42] Slack resources are resources that are in excess of the minimum resources needed for a certain level of output. (Hitt, Ireland & Hoskisson 2007, p. 148) On the one hand, they enable companies to react flexibly. On the other hand, they lock up expensive capital.

As a conclusion about short-termism it can be said that intertemporal trade-offs are inherent in business. Both, short-term and long-term performance is important and should be monitored and evaluated. As shown above, the criticism toward the exclusive use of financial measures is justified.

3.3.3 Sub-optimisation

3.3.3.1 <u>Problem</u>

Sub-optimisation means that objectives of a *sub*-system are pursued to the disadvantage of overall system objectives. Although each sub-system might work at its optimum, this does not have to be true for the system as a whole (Lucey 2003, p. 114). Sub-optimisation in terms of investment can occur if managers can decide over the level of investment – i.e. can decide whether to take an investment opportunity or not – and are evaluated based on return measures.

This leads to different incentives for investing in the same asset across subsidiaries. For example, if an investment opportunity promises a return of 20 percent and subsidiary A currently has an ROI of 40 percent, the manager will be reluctant to invest as it will decrease the subsidiary's overall ROI. However, if subsidiary B is earning a ROI of only 10 percent, it will take the opportunity. The result is that capital is allocated to less successful subsidiaries while there is little or no expansion in highly profitable subsidiaries (Anthony & Govindarajan 2001, pp. 258-259; Merchant & Van der Stede 2007, pp. 447-448).

With the above-mentioned incentive structure, managers of under-performing divisions are furthermore inclined to invest below COC if the investment promises a return below COC but above the current ROI (Merchant & Van der Stede 2007, pp. 447-448).

A related problem is that if a manager can decide over the level of investment, he could theoretically reduce assets to a level at which the company only owns the one asset with the highest return (in percent). However, value (in currency units) is also created with other assets as long as their return is higher than the COC. So, there is an incentive for underinvestment (Jensen & Meckling 2009, p. 53).

3.3.3.2 Possible solutions

A **possible solution** to this problem is to use residual income measures and to make the COC contingent on the respective asset, e.g. by determining required returns for different classes of assets. Thus there is the same profit objective for the same asset company group-wide which means that there is no misallocation of capital and no investing below COC. At the same time, there is an incentive to take every investment with a positive residual income irrespective of the subsidiary's situation as residual income is measured in absolute numbers and cannot spoil average returns.

3.4 Particularities of subsidiary controlling

3.4.1 Overview

3.4.1.1 Using multiple COC rates

From a theoretical standpoint each project that a company undertakes should be analysed at its own discount rate since it has its own inherent risk. If always the company COC was used that would mean that the required return on a very safe investment is equal to the one on a very risky investment. It would also mean that an identical project is rejected by one company and accepted by another company with different COC (Brealey, Myers & Allen 2008, pp. 239-240).

However, in practice company COC is an important figure. First, many projects are standard projects with average risk. Second, company COC is used as a starting point and individual projects' risk is evaluated relative to an average project. Third, a project's true risk is hard to estimate. Fourth, discount rates have motivational implications for managers. (Brealey,

Myers & Allen 2008, pp. 239-240; Borchers 2000, p. 179). Therefore, companies do use standard discount rates.

In company *groups*, the question is at which level the standard discount rates are set. In this thesis it is argued that each subsidiary should have its own discount rate as beta factors largely depend on the industry and thus the SBU (Vogel 1998, p. 117). If a company group includes several subsidiaries in the same industry, one discount rate can be used for a cluster of subsidiaries (Borchers 2006, p. 179). Setting standard discount rates at the level of the subsidiary is consistent with an evaluation of subsidiary managers by performance measures for the entire subsidiary. The subsidiary COC theoretically is an average of the individual projects' COC weighted by their values so that the manager is evaluated by an average of all projects. The corporate COC can be calculated correspondingly from the subsidiaries' COC (Brealey, Myers & Allen 2008, pp. 239-240).

In the calculation of the WACC for a subsidiary, there are three factors whose values have to be determined:

(1) Capital structure
The capital structure assumed in the calculation has a significant influence on the resulting COC. In company groups financing is often coordinated centrally by the holding company so that the actual leverage of subsidiaries can deviate from what is common in the particular industry (Vogel 1998, p. 79; Borchers 2006, p. 178). The debt of individual subsidiaries is often influenced by tax purposes or is "an accident of history" (Koller, Goedhart & Wessels 2005, p. 539). Thus, an industry-typical capital structure, the target group capital structure or the actual group one should be used. If a fictitious capital structure is used, the problem occurs that actual interest expenses do not fit the assumed capital structure. If the group capital structure is used, the differences neutralise in the consolidation. In contrast, with the use of industry-typical or target ones the total fictitious interest expense and value of debt does not fit the actual one at the corporate level. While Vogel (1998, pp. 119-120) argues that the actual capital struc-

tures should be adapted to industry-typical ones, the author of this thesis suggests to use fictitious industry-typical structures for the WACC of subsidiaries and adjust them proportionally so that they match actual group leverage in the consolidated view.

(2) Cost of debt

For the cost of debt average group interest rates can be used as a simplification.

(3) Cost of equity

The cost of equity should be determined separately for each subsidiary. The only element of CAPM that has to be determined separately is beta.

3.4.1.2 Challenges arising from company group affiliation

In this chapter, challenges for the calculation of performance measures in a company group context are *identified*. However, only the first one will be *discussed* in chapter 3.4.2.

A central problem for the calculation of value-based measures is that many subsidiaries are not listed, so that the standard CAPM cannot be applied since no data is available for measuring beta.

Furthermore, there are *intercompany transactions* between the subsidiaries. The question is how these transactions should be dealt with in the evaluation of subsidiary managers, i.e. if the individual subsidiary view or the consolidated company group view is relevant (Burger & Ulbrich 2005, pp. 541-545). The financial situation of individual subsidiaries is furthermore influenced by the transfer pricing policy which is often dominated by tax considerations.

Moreover, it has to be decided how to deal with *corporate costs*, i.e. costs incurred in the corporate centre. They could be allocated to subsidiaries or be retained in the corporate centre if the corporate centre is valuated separately (Koller, Goedhart & Wessels 2005, pp. 532-533).

Additionally, *synergy effects* might be distributed unequally among the subsidiaries so that the financial situation of individual subsidiaries might be distorted.

3.4.1.3 Challenges from subsidiary characteristics

In company groups, there are also challenges in performance measurement that are primarily originated in individual characteristics of the subsidiaries. For a discussion of the problems it is referred to the cited literature.

First, there are *international subsidiaries*. Related problems are for instance differing accounting and taxation regulations, currency translation, currency risks and estimating COC in foreign currency (Koller, Goedhart & Wessels 2005, p. 575ff.). Additionally, in Emerging Markets, particular attention is to be paid to country risks and inflation (Britzelmaier 2010).

Challenges also arise from subsidiaries in a special *stage of their lifecycle* such as start-up companies (Langguth 2008, p. 113ff) or *distressed companies* (Damodaran 2010).

3.4.2 Estimating subsidiary betas

3.4.2.1 Overview on methods

There are different methods which can be used for estimating subsidiary equity betas which can be classified as shown in Figure 11 (Krotter 2008, p. 174; Burger & Ulbrich 2005, p. 551).

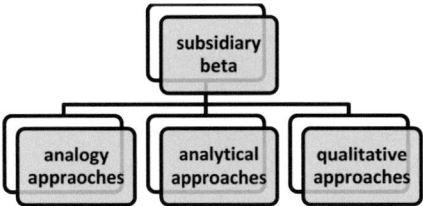

Figure 11: Methods for the estimation of subsidiary betas
Source: Own illustration

(1) Analogy approaches

Analogy approaches – in Anglophone literature often called comparable company approaches (CCA) – use betas of comparable companies as proxies and adjust them for the company-specific leverage. It can be distinguished between three versions: *Pure play beta* uses a single comparable company, *industry beta* uses all companies from the industry and *peer group beta* refers to betas of companies which are comparable in different criteria but not necessarily from the same industry (Burger & Ulbrich 2005, pp. 552-553). With a rising number of companies included in the sample the estimation error drops, but also the comparability between the companies (Bowman & Bush 2006, p. 72)

Once the set of comparable companies has been determined, their equity beta estimates are unlevered in order to obtain the asset beta. Then, a (weighted) average of the asset betas is calculated and re-levered to obtain an estimate of the company's equity beta (Bowman & Bush 2006, p. 73).

The reason for the adjustment of leverage is to remove the impact of *financial* risk. A projects (or company's) *business* risk is independent from its financing. It is measured by the assets beta. If an investor held all securities (equity and debt) of a company, he would only be exposed to the business risk. Therefore the following equation can be used (Brealey, Myers & Allen 2008, p. 543):

$$\beta_{unlevered} = \beta_{assets} = \frac{D}{D+E}\beta_{debt} + \frac{E}{D+E}\beta_{equity}$$

If the equation is solved for β_{equity} and it is assumed that debt is risk free ($\beta_{debt} = 0$) as shown in Appendix 3, the following formula results which is the common formula for levering and unlevering betas by practitioners (Petersen, Plenborg & Schøler 2006, p. 42; Koller, Goedhart & Wessels 2005, p. 712): [43]

$$\beta_{levered(equity)} = \beta_{unlevered(assets)} \left(1 + \frac{D}{E}\right)$$

It can be easily seen that with zero leverage, equity beta is equal to assets beta. With a higher leverage, equity beta increases as returns for shareholders become more risky due to the fixed interest payments.

Betas of comparable companies can be obtained for instance from the financial data provider *Ibbotson Associates* who provides traditional beta estimates as well as 'own products' taking into account other factors besides the correlation with market returns (Pratt 2002, p. 135).

In Appendix 4, the comparable company approach is explained in detail by means of a case study using empirical data of European automotive manufacturers.

(2) Analytical approaches

Analytical approaches try to find out economic determinants of the risk expressed by beta and derive a company's beta from the respective determinants. The determinants can be deduced from theoretical considerations or from empirical data, e.g. by multiple regression analysis (Krotter 2008, p. 175).

In literature, three basic categories of analytical approaches are distinguished between. The first one is *earning beta* which derives beta from a single income figure. The most basic method works correspondingly to

---

[43] There are a number of formulas with different assumptions concerning capital structure and debt riskiness. For an overview cp. Fernández (2003) and Koller et al (2005, p. 713).

regular stock market beta, using accounting income instead of stock returns (Pfister 2003, p. 147).

$$\beta_{subsidiary} = \frac{cov(income_{subsidiary}; income_{market})}{var(income_{market})}$$

The second category is *accounting beta* which takes into account more than one accounting measure. An example is the so-called operating leverage which derives beta from the proportion of fixed and variable costs. The economic argumentation is that if fixed costs are high, changes in sales lead to comparably larger changes in profit and return, i.e. return is more volatile (Pfister 2003, pp. 167-170).

Third, there are *fundamental beta* approaches which are more elaborate approaches taking into account a variety of data (Pfister 2003, p. 133; Burger & Ulbrich 2005, p. 555).

(3) Qualitative approaches

Qualitative approaches do not establish a quantitative connection between the determinants of risk and the beta factor but a rather subjective one (Krotter 2008, p. 175; Pfister 2003, p. 221).

One qualitative method are *management estimates* in which managers are asked to estimate the SBU's risk for instance based on an evaluation if the risk is higher or lower than the risk of other companies or industries with known beta factors (Pfister 2003, pp. 222-223).

Furthermore, there are *scoring models* which evaluate the risk of the subsidiary by several criteria. The total score results in an adjustment of the beta of a comparable company (Weißenberger 2007, pp. 305-306; Krotter 2008, p. 175).

Please note that only approaches which estimate betas, i.e. which are compatible with the CAPM were discussed above. There are also approaches which directly estimate the cost of equity. In particular there are

risk components approaches – also called build-up models – which add
risk premiums for different factors to the risk-free. For instance *Ibbotson
Associates* provides data on risk premiums for equity risk, firm size and
industry based on empirical financial market data (Pratt 2002, p. 119).
Sometimes also subjective premiums are added to the risk-free rate, e.g.
for lack of marketability (Pfister 2003, p. 223; Petersen, Plenborg &
Schøler 2006, p. 44). Besides the build-up models there is a variety of
other pragmatic approaches – often developed by consultancies. An example is the approach of *Boston Consulting Group* which is based on a
scoring model and adjusts the overall corporate COC rate depending on
the subsidiary's score (Burger & Ulbrich 2005, pp. 556-557).

3.4.2.2 Evaluation and discussion of the methods

Analogy approaches have become the standard method for measuring
betas of non-listed companies. However, there is limited empirical research on their usefulness (Bowman & Bush 2006, p. 71). The main problem of the approaches is how to determine comparable companies. For
smaller companies it is often hard to find a comparable company (Krotter
2008, pp. 174-175; Petersen, Plenborg & Schøler 2006, p. 41).

The advantage of *analytical approaches* is that no comparable company
needs to be found. Additionally, they are very plausible and economically
justifiable. Moreover, it is even possible to forecast the determinants for
the future and thus calculate a future-oriented beta (which is not possible
by means of a regular beta calculation from financial market data). However, the central problem is the choice of determinants of risk. It is also
questionable if the determinants are the same for different companies
(Burger & Ulbrich 2005, pp. 555-556; Krotter 2008, p. 175).

Qualitative approaches are rejected in this thesis due to the lack of theoretical, statistical and empirical foundation (Burger & Ulbrich 2005, p. 557).
However, it is recognised that they are important in practice if there is not
enough data available for analogy or analytical approaches. It is also rec-

ognised that a main advantage of them is that they can be applied in a more future-oriented way.

In a survey by Petersen, Plenborg & Schøler (2006) among Danish financial advisers and private equity funds, it resulted that analogy approaches are the most used method among the participants (68 percent) whereas analytical approaches were only used by 32 percent. 56 percent stated that they also include their personal experience (multiple choices possible). In a German study by Drukarczyk & Schüler it also turned out that peer group estimates are the most applied method (Weißenberger 2007, p. 305).

In general, it is recommendable to combine several approaches – at least for plausibility checks (Weißenberger 2007, p. 307; Burger & Ulbrich 2005, p. 558).

3.5 Concluding discussion of financial measures

In the table below, the discussion of the financial measures from the previous chapters is summarised in terms of the evaluation criteria and also the dysfunctions and biases. The measures are evaluated on a scale ranging from negative (-) to positive (+).

Measures			Evaluation										
			control-relevance			decision-relevance			subsidiary		dysfunctions / biases		
			congruence	controllability	objectivity	timeliness	analysability	consideration of risk	comparability	aggregation	age bias	short-termism	sub-optimisation
Measures	Traditional	Profit	-	+	o	o	o	-	-	+	+	-	o
		CF	o	+	+	o	o	-	-	+	+	-	o
		ROI	-	+	o	o	o	-	+	o	-	-	-
	Value-based	EVA	o	o	o	o	+	+	-	-	-	-	+
		CFROI	o	o	+	o	o	+	+	o	+	-	-
	Capital market	Return	o	-	+	o	-	-	+	o	+	o	o
		SR	o	-	+	o	-	+	+	-	+	o	o

Figure 12: Concluding evaluation of financial measures (by criteria)
Source: Own illustration

The table could also be converted into a scoring model by translating the qualitative scale into a quantitative scale and weighting the evaluation criteria according to the individual needs derived from the company and the purpose of measurement.

In Figure 13 on page 69, the distribution of the values is shown for each performance measure. Under the premise of an equal weighting of the criteria, the following conclusions can be drawn: Among the traditional measures, CF seems to be superior while CFROI seems to be the best value-based measure. For capital market-based measures, there is no clear winner which is better in both '+' and 'o' count.

Furthermore, it can be stated that no measure is perfect, so that a combination of different *financial* measures makes sense which mutually neutralise their weaknesses, for instance CFROI and SR.

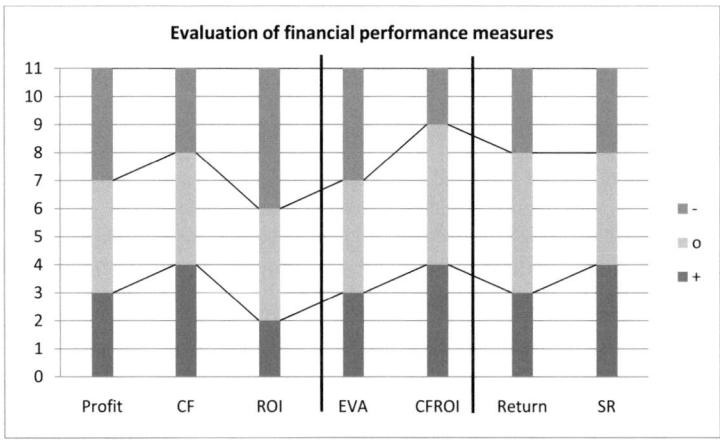

Figure 13: Concluding evaluation of financial measures (total)
Source: Own illustration

Moreover, in this part of the thesis it was shown that the criticism against financial measures is in part justified. It was also shown how dysfunctions and biases can be alleviated by adjusting the measures and using correctly. However, not all problems can be completely relieved. Therefore, it can be stated that combinations of financial and non-financial measures do make sense, too.

Still, as Chow & Van der Stede (2006, p. 7) state, one needs to "be cautious about popular claims that non-financial measures are superior to traditional financial measures across the board. Rather than being an either/or choice, the challenge is to select the optimal combination".

4 Performance measurement systems as an entity

4.1 Contingency in designing PMS

4.1.1 Theoretical and conceptual fundament

4.1.1.1 An outline of contingency theory

Before contingency theory emerged in the 1950s, the prevailing notion of traditional organisational and management theory was that certain principles are universally applicable to all circumstances (Kieser & Kubicek 1992, p. 47; Jackson 2000, p. 110). Contingency theory – which was primarily oriented toward organisational design – argues that there is no best way of structuring an organisation (Morgan 1998, p. 44; Jackson 2000, p. 110). Instead, the optimal design depends on situational factors (also referred to as contingent factors or contextual factors) since they impose constraints on the organisation (Drury 2004, pp. 695-696; Jackson 2000, p. 110).

The design of formal structures depending on the context is assumed to have an influence on the effectiveness and efficiency of an organisation (Jackson 2000, p. 110; Kieser & Walgenbach 2007, p. 43). Therefore, management should be concerned with aligning contingent variables and the system in order to achieve good fits (Morgan 1998, p. 44; Drury 2004, p. 696).

In the meantime, the application of contingency theory has been extended to a variety of management fields such as motivation and leadership (Wunderer 2007, pp. 311-313) and also management accounting and information systems (Otley 1980, p. 413)

4.1.1.2 The contingency approach to PMS and subsidiary controlling

Also the design of **PMS** should depend on situational factors. Hence the model presented in Figure 14 will be used for the contingent design of PMS. It has to be emphasised though that a PMS must be designed in the context of an overall organisational control system and has to be congruent with the other sub-systems which will be discussed later.

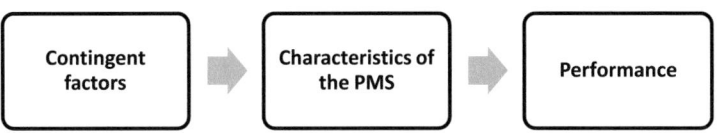

Figure 14: The contingency model of PMS design
Source: With adaptations from Otley (1980, pp.420-421) and Drury (2004, p. 697)

In terms of **subsidiary controlling**, contingency approach can mean two different things: A *company group-specific* or a *subsidiary-specific* subsidiary controlling. The first possibility means that the general design of subsidiary controlling is made contingent on context factors *of the company group* as for instance Maier (2001) does in his dissertation. The second possibility is also discussed under the keyword *standardisation vs. differentiation.* By differentiation, it is meant that the characteristics of subsidiary controlling should not be universal across the company group but designed individually *for each subsidiary* depending on the respective situational factors (Borchers 2006, p. 238).

While in practice, a growing standardisation of subsidiary controlling can be observed (Kremer 2008, p. 172) academics often call for a differentiated subsidiary controlling (Borchers 2000, p. 66; Horváth 1997, p. 83; Kremer 2008, p. 172). The main justification of a subsidiary-specific controlling is that local peculiarities, for instance arising from national culture or history can be taken into account. Otherwise, wrong control signals might be sent and subsidiary's management might not follow corporate objectives. On the other hand, standardisation of subsidiary controlling provides cost advantages as less time and effort is required for coordination of standardised processes in the corporate centre. Additionally, comparability between subsidiaries is higher if they are controlled in the same way (Ewert & Wagenhofer 2000, p. 58; Hoffjan & Weide 2006, p. 392).

So there is a continuum between standardisation and differentiation on which each company group has to find its optimal point. To do so, there are theoretical cost-oriented models which take into account the advantages of standardisation as cost savings and the disadvantages as costs (Hoffjan 2009, p. 273).

Subsequently, a company group-specific and subsidiary-specific subsidiary controlling is represented. In a second step, company groups can form clusters of subsidiaries with similar characteristics and standardise subsidiary controlling within the clusters as Vogel (1998, pp. 133-137) suggests.

4.1.2 Research and methodological issues

4.1.2.1 Contingency approaches in research

Contingency theory literature can be classified into two strands: Authors from the *theoretical strand* speculate or hypothesise on possible contextual factors. This type of research provides input for subsequent empirical studies. In contrast, *empirical research* intends to figure out an appropriate match between organisational design and the contextual factors empirically. Most empirical studies are based on questionnaires (Drury 2004, pp. 696-697).

Empirical studies involve lots of difficulties. A major problem in empirically testing a theory which only deals with one sub-system of management control is the isolation from other organisational controls. Thus there is the danger of model underspecification, i.e. several controls influence the behaviour of employees but the result is only blamed to part of the control system (Chenhall 2003, p. 131). Further problems are the enormous number of possible factors, as well as the definition and measurement of abstract variables. This measurement problem not only occurs for the contingent factors but also for the outcome (performance). Additionally, there is a potential of drawing wrong conclusions from observed correlations since they might be merely statistical correlations instead of economic causalities (Chenhall 2003, pp. 135-136; Drury 2004, p. 697).

Empirical studies differ in terms of what the dependent and independent variable is. Arising from the difficulties in measuring performance, there are so-called *selection studies* which only examine the relationship between contextual factors and the control system of companies without addressing the question whether a certain combination leads to a better performance (Chenhall 2003, p. 155). That means they only examine the relationship between the first two boxes of Figure 14. Critics claim that studies should include performance as the dependent variable (Chenhall 2003, p. 135). Proponents of such studies, however, argue that rational managers will not employ systems which do not enhance performance so that insights about the adoption of systems in practice do provide helpful insights (Drury 2004, p. 698; Chenhall 2003, p. 135). They use simple correlations or linear regression without taking into account the relationship between various contextual factors (Chenhall 2003, p. 155).

Interaction approaches use situational factors as moderating variable in order to see how it influences the relationship between control system elements and performance. Moderating variables can also be combined with intervening models in order to separate direct and indirect effects on the outcome by specifying causal paths between different variables (Chenhall 2003, p. 155).

System approaches test multiple fits between variables simultaneously and how performance varies with different combinations. The statistical models used (e.g. Euclidean distance or cluster analysis) require large sample sizes (Chenhall 2003, pp. 155-156).

4.1.2.2 Further proceeding in this thesis

After some general issues of PMS design will be pointed out in the rest of chapter 4, in chapter 5 contextual factors and their influence on PMS design will be presented.

Up to this point, no sharp definition of contextual factor has been presented yet. While Otley (1980, p. 421) considers contextual factors to be outside of the organisation's control, Littkemann & Derfuß (2009, pp. 32-33) distinguish between external factors that cannot be influenced and internal factors that can be influenced. In this thesis, no clear statement about the possibility to influence contextual factors is made. Instead of assuming unidirectional relationships it is argued – following the idea of systems theory – that there is mutual influence between the PMS and the contextual factors as visualised in Figure 15. For example, when designing PMS, the organisational culture should be considered. In a culture of mutual trust, very tight controls can have negative influences. On the other hand, an introduced PMS can also shape the existing culture to a certain degree.

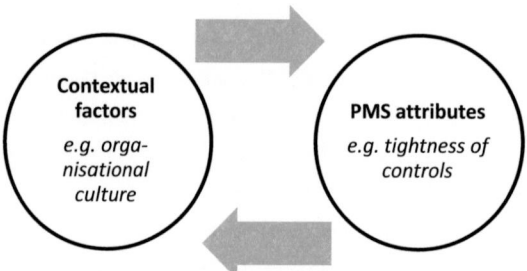

Figure 15: Mutual influence between PMS and contextual factors
Source: With adaptations from Bititci et al (2006, p. 1326)

Sometimes it even cannot be clearly said whether a certain variable is a contextual factor or an attribute of the PMS. This especially depends on the definition of the control system and the determination of system boundaries. For instance decentralisation is considered a choice in the control system design by Abernethy et al (2004) while Chenhall (2003) considers it to be a contextual factor.

If it is tried to fit the used methodology of this thesis into the classification of research above, it belongs to the *theoretical strand* hypothesising on the matches between PMS attributes and contextual factors. Thus, a lack of empirical evidence could be criticised. However, empirical results from several studies are included. Furthermore, it could be criticised that there is the risk of model underspecification as explained above. However, the term PMS is defined comparably broadly in this thesis so that interrelated elements such as incentives are included. Moreover, related sub-systems of the MCS are taken into account in the contextual factors so that a holistic proceeding is ensured.

4.1.3 Dynamic evolution of PMS

Already in the late 1960s, Drucker (The Age of Discontinuity: Guidelines to Our Changing Society 1969, pp. ix-xi) called out the 'age of discontinuity' predicting major changes in the areas of technology, world economy, society and knowledge. In the meantime, it has been commonly stated that the environment in which organisations operate is increasingly dynamic (Hoque 2003, p. 44; Kennerley & Neely 2003, p. 215; Horváth 2006, p. 3).

This requires an ongoing modification of strategies and operations, but also of the organisation and control systems which have to be flexible and adaptive (Kennerley & Neely 2003, p. 213; Horváth 2006, p. 10). While companies seem to have understood the importance of a contingent design of control systems at the point of implementation, there is still potential for improvement in terms of actively managing the systems in order to make sure that they are still in line with the contextual variables as they change (Kennerley & Neely 2003, p. 215).

Kennerley & Neely (2003) have developed a (quite intuitive) model to manage the evolution of PMS which will not be discussed in detail. However, it is emphasised that it is crucial to continue to reflect on the individual measures, the PMS as an entity and the supporting infrastructure in order to check if they still meet the requirements. This can be done on a regular basis or as external triggers imply changes.

4.2 Features of PMS

4.2.1 Integration for successful performance management

4.2.1.1 <u>Performance measurement vs. performance management</u>

In this chapter, the importance of seeing PMS as management systems instead of mere measurement systems is emphasised. Academics criticise that research has recently paid too much attention to ex post performance measurement instead of ex ante management (Broadbent & Laughlin 2009, p. 283). This problem especially occurs with VBM systems. If they are mistaken as mere ex post measures, they do not help improve performance substantially (Koller, Goedhart & Wessels 2005, pp. 406-407).[44]

In terms of VBM, instead of measuring performance ex post it must be made sure that in each decision that is made in daily business, the goal of value creation is considered (Koller, Goedhart & Wessels 2005, p. 405). Effective performance management thus requires a thorough understanding of the underlying factors that influence value creation.

The word 'integrated' has not found its way into the thesis' title by chance. Integration is the key to an effective design of PMS. It is defined as *creation of unity* or *inclusion into a larger whole* (Gabler Wirtschaftslexikon 2010). It can be both an act and a condition. In terms of PMS, integration should be attained in various dimensions which will be explained in the following chapter.

---

[44] Consequently, the term performance *management* systems would better describe the systems as explained in this thesis. However, the term performance *measurement* system has grown from history and thus still prevails in literature.

Besides the design of the system 'soft' factors or – as Koller et al (2005, p. 408) formulate it – the "rigor and honesty" of the process play an important role. This includes establishing a value creation mind-set in the organisational culture. Once the system is established, the communication between the management levels should not be confined to checking whether a certain target has been reached and who is to blame for deviations. Instead, deviations should be analysed and concrete steps for improvement should be discussed (Koller, Goedhart & Wessels 2005, p. 424).

4.2.1.2 Dimensions of integration

Above all, integration of PMS refers to integration of various systems in the organisation (Bititci, Carrie & McDevitt 1997, pp. 526-527). In general, it can be said that each sub-system should be designed in a way that it is congruent with both the other systems on the same level and its super-system (Jackson 2000, p. 110). Referring to the used model in this thesis, the first level of integration between systems is *between the sub-systems of the PMS*. In literature, especially a link between performance measures and compensation is demanded (Jensen & Meckling 2009, p. 49; Gleich 2001, pp. 24-25). Otherwise, the measurement does not result in any behaviour changes (Koller, Goedhart & Wessels 2005, p. 407).

The second level of systems integration is *between the PMS and the other sub-systems of its super-system MCS*. Especially an integration with the general operational and strategic planning and control system as shown in chapter 2 is important (Gleich 2001, p. 22). Otherwise, the planning of performance would be separate from actual business.

Related to this, the PMS should be integrated with *strategy* by deriving its design from strategic objectives. Otherwise, it would support activities that are contrary to what strategy demands (Tangen 2004, p. 727). Anthony & Govindarajan (2001, p. 441) see implementing strategy as the main objective of PMS. Besides merely implementing strategy, PMS can even help the company to improve its strategic position if they are truly integrated with strategic planning (Hoque 2003, p. 142). This can be achieved due to two mechanisms. First, PMS align the organisation's activities with its objectives. This is done by breaking down objectives which will be shown in the next chapter. Second, PMS contribute to organisational learning by supplying information that provides an understanding of cause-effect relationships between operations and strategy (Chenhall 2005, p. 396).

For the implementation of strategy, an integration of *financial and non-financial performance measure* that cover *different perspectives* is necessary. In combination, they enable management to translate strategy into performance measures (Chenhall 2005, p. 396). This principle is well-known from the BSC which is an example for a comprehensive PMS that fulfils the requirements demanded in this chapter.

Moreover, PMS of different *organisational units* should be integrated throughout different organisational dimensions, for instance functional areas or regions. In terms of subsidiary controlling, the PMS should be integrated over all levels of the company group. This is especially an issue for recently acquired subsidiaries.

In practice, the integration of PMS of different organisational units is often an *information systems* issue. Integrated information technology (IT) infrastructure prevents the company from time-consuming data collection, sorting and reporting (Bititci, Nudurupati & Turner 2002, p. 1275). This is particularly relevant if there are legacy systems, i.e. historically grown systems in subsidiaries which are incompatible with the main system of the company group. In this case, the legacy system has to be integrated with the management information system (MIS) used for reporting. It has to be decided if it is replaced or how the interfaces an be designed.

It has been shown, that integration is crucial in order for PMS to be effective. However, it should not be confused with standardisation as the individual situation of the subsidiaries still has to be taken into account.

4.2.2 Breaking down objectives

4.2.2.1 Operationalisation

As previously noted, PMS are an enhancement of traditional target planning in terms of formulating targets with reference to persons and objects. The process of breaking down a company's vision to performance measures as shown in Figure 16 is also referred to as *deployment* (Bititci, Carrie & McDevitt 1997, p. 524).

Figure 16: The deployment process
Source: Own illustration based on Kaplan & Norton (2001, p. 73) and Bititci et al (1997, p. 524)

There is a "logical continuum" (Kaplan & Norton 2001, pp. 69-72) that ranges from the company's mission to its performance measures. The abstract mission must be translated so that it operationalised. This process continues until it is broken down to activities performed by employees. Thus their actions are aligned and support the company's mission.

In the BSC, the cause-and-effect logic which links the performance measures with the more abstract objectives located higher in the continuum is described in so-called strategy maps (Kaplan & Norton 2001, pp. 69-72).

In the context of VBM so-called *value drivers* and *value metrics* have to be identified on the performance measure level. Value drivers are activities that affect performance and thereby create value. Value metrics are measures that quantify how well it is performed in terms of the value drivers. The top 10 to 15 value metrics are referred to as key performance indicators (KPI) (Koller, Goedhart & Wessels 2005, p. 410).

It has to be clear to management which value drivers are fundamental to the performance. Only if it is succeeded in breaking down the objective of value creation to all decision levels, a reliable VBM can be implemented. Otherwise, it appears as mere window-dressing for analysts (Britzelmaier 2009, p. 168). Therefore, a systematic process for identifying value drivers at all levels has to be established (Koller, Goedhart & Wessels 2005, p. 408).

A proven method for operationalisation is to use so-called *value trees* which operationalise the top value-based measure in a top-down approach (Britzelmaier 2009, p. 173). Koller et al (2005, pp. 411-417) suggest doing so in a two-step approach: First, the metrics are broken down until each measure of financial performance is translated into an operational metric. Next, value drivers – i.e. activities – are associated with the metrics. In a second step, the KPIs are identified by prioritising the value drivers. This is necessary since management cannot focus on all value drivers. Additionally, it helps to decide which value drivers are pursued if there are trade-offs and to concentrate on activities which have the largest positive effect on value. Which value drivers are relevant depends on several factors such as the company's industry and strategy. For instance, with a premium strategy, different value drivers are important than with a low-cost strategy.

Tools that support the management of identified KPIs are *dashboards*. They display the KPIs in a condensed form and often in real time which allows management to get an overview and realise the need for interventions quickly. There is a variety of commercial software solutions, for instance IBM Cognos Business Intelligence or SAP Business Objects which allow easy access via web browsers (Ballou, Heitger & Donnell 2010, p. 30).[45]

4.2.2.2 Considerations concerning subsidiary controlling

Besides operationalising value creation in a value tree, the measures have to be broken down to lower-level organisational units (Britzelmaier 2009, p. 175). Thus, it can be said that breaking down objectives is carried out two-dimensionally: deployment and delegation.

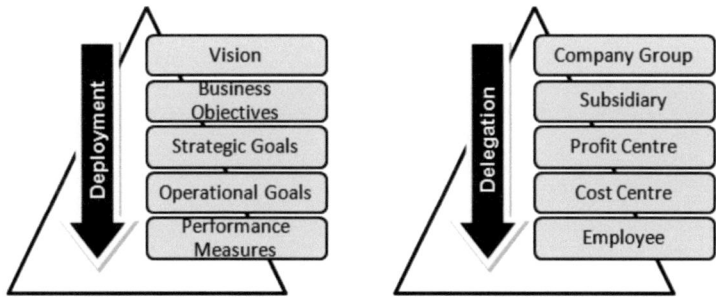

Figure 17: Breaking down objectives two-dimensionally
Source: Own illustration based on Kaplan & Norton (2001, p. 73), Bititci et al (1997, p. 524) and Britzelmaier (2009, p. 176)

Two comments have to be made about Figure 17. First, the organisational units which objectives are delegated to are just illustrative and can vary depending on the organisational structure. Second, elements from one dimension cannot be exclusively designed to one element of the other dimension, i.e. it is not necessarily the case that delegation is accompanied by deployment and vice versa. For instance both the company group as a whole and subsidiaries can have a vision and also the corporate centre can use operationalised performance measures.

The question in subsidiary controlling is down to which level the corporate centre intervenes in the two dimensions. In terms of delegation, does it

---

[45] It is renounced on a comprehensive discussion of dashboards in terms of their advantages and disadvantages. For a discussion of challenges cp. Ballou et al (2010).

only set targets for the subsidiary as a whole or also for lower-level organisational units? In terms of deployment, corporate centres will set quantitative targets for performance measures. However, this could be limited to an aggregated financial measure or be further broken down to non-aggregated financial or even operational measures in the value tree. The answer to these questions depends on the contextual factors and will be discussed later.

5 Contextual factors of performance measurement systems

5.1 Introduction

5.1.1 Classification of and overview on possible factors

The classification of contextual factors is adopted from Borchers (2000, pp. 60-61) who states that they can be classified according to two dimensions: *internal vs. external* and *company group-specific vs. subsidiary-specific*. External factors cannot be exclusively assigned to either the company group or subsidiary so that they are only classified according to one dimension. An overview on possible factors of the different categories can be seen in Figure 18 (in alphabetical order, not mutually exclusive).

external	internal	
	company group-specific	subsidiary-specific
dynamics of the environm.	corporate culture	business strategy
economic environment	corporate philosophy	economic situation
national culture	corporate strategy	industry/product
political/legal environment	decentralisation	legal form
socio-cultural environment	information asymmetry	location
technological environment	interdependences	mgmt. qualification
environmental uncertainty	internationalisation	organisation life cycle
	organisational structure	participation quota
	size	size
		strategic role
		subsidiary life cycle
		technology

Figure 18: Overview on contextual factors
Source of contents: Borchers (2000, p. 62) and Chenhall (2003)

In this thesis, not all factors can be dealt with. The intention is to give examples how the contextual factors can influence the design of PMS. Subsequently, two company group-specific and two subsidiary-specific internal factors will be discussed in detail, namely corporate strategy, organisational structure of the company group, business strategy of the subsidiary and size of the subsidiary.

5.1.2 Relationships between factors

The contextual factors will be presented separately from each other for systematic reasons. However, one has to be aware of the fact that there are also interdependences between the contextual factors (Borchers 2000, p. 64). This fact is illustrated in Figure 19 (red arrows) using the contextual factors presented in this thesis and uncertainty as an additional external factor as an example.

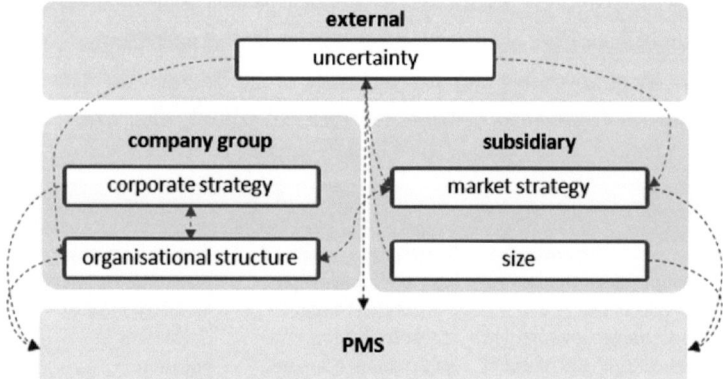

Figure 19: Relationships between contextual factors
Source: Own illustration

The interdependence between the contextual factors has the following consequence for PMS design: If the company's internal contextual factors have not been designed consistently (for instance strategy and organisational structure), problems for PMS design occur. This is because certain contextual factors imply a particular design of PMS (blue arrows in the picture). If the contextual factors are not consistent, one factor might imply a different PMS design than another. This again highlights the importance of integration of all of a company's sub-systems which should theoretically be designed simultaneously.[46]

---

[46] Abernethy et al (2004) apply a simultaneous quantitative model where decentralisation and the use of performance measures are mutually dependent.

An example for mutual influence is *organisational structure* and *corporate strategy*: On the one hand, it is assumed that there is an optimal organisational structure for a certain corporate strategy ('structure follows strategy'). More precisely, diversified companies are supposed to be more decentralised. On the other hand, it can also be argued that once a certain structure is in place, strategic decisions might be influenced by organisational structure, for instance because a decentralised organisation offers better opportunities for diversification ('strategy follows structure') (Chenhall 2003, pp. 144-145).

Another example is the *business strategy* and *uncertainty*: On the one hand, the level of uncertainty in the environment might influence the choice of an adequate strategy (Hoque 2004, p. 486). On the other hand, certain business strategies are associated with a higher level of uncertainty. More specific, strategies which focus on growth and innovation involve a higher level of uncertainty than more conservative strategies (Shank & Govindarajan 1992).

5.2 Company group-specific factors

5.2.1 Corporate strategy

5.2.1.1 Introduction

Corporate strategy – also referred to as diversification strategy – is primarily concerned with questions of choosing businesses to be in and allocating resources. A company group's corporate strategy can be classified into three categories on a continuum ranging from no diversification to a high degree of diversification (Verbeeten 2005, p. 13; Merchant & Van der Stede 2007, p. 726):

Single business organisations only operate in one line of business while *related diversified* organisations diversify within the scope of their core competences in order to benefit from synergy effects. In contrast *unrelated diversified companies* which have mainly a finance background are not necessarily familiar with the different businesses. The corporate centre functions as a holding company and primarily engages in investment and financing activities. The holding expects to earn large returns on the investment in the subsidiaries (Verbeeten 2005, pp. 13-14; Merchant & Van der Stede 2007, p. 726).

As single business organisations are not within the scope of this thesis (cp. chapter 2.1.1) only the differences between related diversified and unrelated diversified companies will be discussed subsequently.

5.2.1.2 Consequences for PMS design

(1) Choice of performance measures

Corporate centres of *unrelated diversified* companies are not necessarily familiar with the business of their subsidiaries. Due to the information asymmetry they might not be able to correctly implement and interpret non-financial measures. Another problem of non-financial measures in this context is that they are not comparable between subsidiaries of different industries since they are likely to have differing critical success factors so that non-financial measures are of limited usefulness. Hence, unrelated diversified companies heavily rely on financial measures. Especially value-based measures are commonly used. Even if they do use non-financial measures, their PMS are dominated by common measures that can be applied corporate-wide as opposed to unique measures tailored to the respective businesses (Verbeeten 2005, pp. 13-14; Merchant & Van der Stede 2007, p. 726).

As corporate centres of *related diversified* companies are supposedly familiar with the business of the different subsidiaries, they can include non-financial measures in their PMS. Also, they do not affect comparability of results as the subsidiaries are all engaged in similar business so that they are likely to have the same KPIs. Another argument in favour of non-aggregated measures brought up by Abernethy et al (2004, p. 562) is that if there are interdependencies between subsidiaries – which is the case if synergies are supposed to be exploited – aggregated financial measures on the subsidiary-level are noisy since they might be influenced by other subsidiaries' performance.

It has to be emphasised that the strong use of financial measures in *unrelated diversified* companies is not a recommendation but rather an empirically observable phenomenon (Verbeeten 2005, pp. 13-14). Hence, companies should be aware of the fact that subsidiary managers are likely to engage in dysfunctional behaviour if they are only evaluated by financial measures. Especially short-termism and sub-optimisation are an issue so that in the choice and design of financial measures the principles pointed out in chapter 0 should be taken into account.

(2) Incentives design

As *related diversified* companies intend to benefit from synergies, the PMS should be designed in a way that makes exploitation of synergies possible. In order to motivate subsidiary managers to consider synergies, Merchant & Van der Stede (2007, p. 727) suggest to make a part of the subsidiary managers' compensation dependent on the performance of the next higher-level entity in the company, i.e. for instance of an intermediate holding company or the overall company group.

In contrast, it makes little sense for *unrelated diversified* companies to tie bonuses to corporate performance since this is a very noisy measure if the subsidiaries are only very loosely connected. In order to alleviate short-termism, an extension of the measurement horizon, i.e. a reduction of the frequency of bonus payments might make sense.

(3) Planning and control process

In order to be able to exploit synergies, *related diversified* often have quite elaborate planning and budgeting systems. Besides their primary purpose, they have the secondary effect that they force managers from different subsidiaries to communicate and coordinate their activities. Moreover, transfer pricing issues are important if there are strong links between several subsidiaries in order to show a 'correct' financial result of all units (Merchant & Van der Stede 2007, p. 727; Abernethy, Bouwens & Van Lent 2004, p. 562).

In *unrelated diversified* companies, there is a tendency to evaluate managers formally by objective measures with little subjective judgment involved. This increases pressure for financial results even more (Merchant & Van der Stede 2007, p. 727). Hence, a correct design of the financial measures in order to alleviate dysfunctional behaviour becomes even more important.

5.2.2 Organisational Structure

5.2.2.1 Introduction

In German literature on subsidiary controlling, organisational structures of company groups are often classified into three types: integrated company group, management holding company and financial holding company[47] (Kremer 2008, pp. 46-48; Burger & Ulbrich 2005, pp. 65-72). The typology is presented under different headlines (for example corporate centre roles, leadership types and organisational structures) and there are different criteria for distinguishing between the three types (Burger & Ulbrich 2005, p. 67). However, it can be said that the main difference between the types is the level of decentralisation. While the integrated company group is operationally integrated – i.e. the corporate centre is involved in operational business –, decisions and tasks in the financial holding company are largely delegated to the local entities.

Also in contingency research, a main question concerning organisational structure is how the level of decentralisation affects the design of control systems (Littkemann 2009a, p. 83; Chenhall 2006, p. 97). Subsequently, it

---

[47] German: *Stammhauskonzern / integrierter Konzern, Managementholding* and *Finanzholding*.

will be shown how the general level of decentralisation affects the design of the PMS. As the author considers decentralisation to be a continuous (as opposed to discrete) criterion, the three-step German typology is not used in the following. Rather, decentralisation is seen as a continuum.[48]

5.2.2.2 Consequences for PMS design

(1) Choice of performance measures

Decentralisation particularly has an influence on the level of aggregation of performance measures (Chenhall 2003, p. 147). Aggregation of measures should always follow the controllability principle as discussed in chapter 3, that means it should reflect the decision rights that were delegated. It is clear that managers should not be made responsible for factor which they cannot control. On the other hand, Abernethy et al (2004, p. 548) state that measures used to evaluate subsidiary managers should be as aggregated as possible. They argue that the use of non-aggregated measures would transfer responsibility back to the corporate centre as subsidiary management would not have to make trade-offs among various activities that are measured in order to optimise the subsidiary's total performance.

Furthermore, concerning non-financial measures it might be difficult for the corporate centre to decompose the measures to lower levels within the subsidiaries (Chenhall 2006, p. 110). Therefore, in this thesis it is suggested to evaluate subsidiary managers in decentralised organisations by aggregated financial measures – especially value-based measures – and to delegate breaking down the objectives to lower levels to them. Corporate centre could assume the role of a consultant in the process.

This notion is in line with German subsidiary controlling literature suggesting that in decentralised organisational structures subsidiaries are evalu-

---

[48] It could also be argued that decentralisation is a subsidiary-specific factor. Here, it is assumed that the level of decentralisation is a general policy decision of the company group and only varies insignificantly among subsidiaries.

ated by financial summary measures. With increasing centralisation, market share targets, functional area targets and as a last step process targets are used (Littkemann 2009a, p. 83).

In terms of particular types of performance measures which can be used, decentralisation especially affects the controllability of value-based measures whereas non-financial measures are considered to be very controllable (Chenhall 2006, p. 101).

(2) Incentives design

In order to reflect the increased authority of subsidiary managers in decentralised organisations, a greater part of their compensation can be variable.

(3) Planning and control process

In more decentralised organisations, there is a stronger emphasis on formal processes and more administrative controls, i.e. performance planning is more sophisticated and there a more formal patterns of communication (Chenhall 2003, p. 146).

With an increasing delegation of decisions and tasks to lower entities the need for coordination and alignment with corporate goals increases, too (Littkemann 2009a, p. 83). This can be taken into account by higher levels of participation of subsidiary managers in the performance planning process (Chenhall 2006, p. 97).

5.3 Subsidiary-specific factors

5.3.1 Business strategy

5.3.1.1 Introduction

The demarcation of subsidiaries in terms of product-market combinations as discussed previously makes clear that the business strategy is to be discussed on the subsidiary level as different subsidiaries may employ different strategies. Strategy is a particularly important contextual factor because of the strategic orientation of integrated PMS and their role as a tool for the implementation of strategy as discussed in chapter 4.

Strategies of SBUs can be classified in a variety of ways. Here, besides Porter's (1985, p. 61) *generic strategies of low cost, differentiation and focus* which are assumed to be known, two concepts which are of particular interest in contingency research will be presented: *Defenders, prospectors and analysers* which was introduced by Miles and Snow as well as *build, hold, harvest and divest* which is especially promoted by the Indian-American professor Govindarajan (Hoque 2004, pp. 487-488; Verbeeten 2005, pp. 15-16). In a contingency context, many researchers reduce the concepts to a continuum between two extreme poles. This has among others the advantage that the strategy can be quantified on a Likert-type scale – for instance ranging from 1 (harvest) to 5 (build) – in empirical research. This simplification will also be made in this thesis, so that the typologies result which are shown in Figure 20.

Figure 20: SBU strategy typologies
Source: Own illustration

Subsidiaries with a *build* strategy have above all the goal of increasing market share, even at the expense of short-term financial performance. They are likely to be cross-subsidised by other subsidiaries. The *harvest* strategy implies maximising short-term earnings and cash flows. Harvesting subsidiaries are net suppliers of cash (Shank & Govindarajan 1992, p. 15).

Prospector firms are looking for opportunities in the market and try to maintain their reputation of being an innovator. *Defenders* define a segment of the market and try to defend their stable domain. They attempt to produce and distribute products as efficiently as possible in their narrow segment (Miles et al. 1978, pp. 550-552).

5.3.1.2 Consequences for PMS design

The specifics of control systems *for build, prospector and differentiation strategies* are similar to each other. The same is true for *harvest, defender and low cost strategies.* This is especially because they face a comparable level of uncertainty (Shank & Govindarajan 1992, pp. 16, 21).

Furthermore, they have the same implications for short-term versus long-term profit trade-offs. Build, prospector and differentiation strategies for instance tend to include large R&D expenses which decrease short-term profit (Shank & Govindarajan 1992, pp. 16, 21). In order to ensure the long-term focus of such strategies, particular attention has to be paid to the solutions against short-termism as discussed in chapter 3.3.2.

Consequently, for the further proceeding of this chapter, the strategies are classified into two new categories according to their implications for PMS design as shown in Figure 21.

Figure 21: Control system design classification of strategy typologies
Source: Own illustration

(1) Choice of performance measures

Companies of the *PMS Design 1 type* are likely to have critical success factors such as a high level of innovation, creativity and staff involvement (Merchant & Van der Stede 2007, p. 728; Shank & Govindarajan 1992, p. 20). Besides difficulties to express these factors in financial terms, an excessive use of financial measures might influence managers to neglect these factors as investments in the factors only pay off in the long run (Hoque 2004, p. 488). Therefore, more emphasis should be placed on non-financial measures compared to firms of the PMS Design 2 type (Verbeeten 2005, p. 16; Hoque 2004, p. 488; Shank & Govindarajan 1992, p. 19). Additionally, these factors might even be difficult to measure with non-financial measures, so that they might have to be evaluated subjectively (Verbeeten 2005, p. 16; Merchant & Van der Stede 2007, p. 728).

In contrast, companies of the *PMS Design 2 type* should rather focus on financial performance. Especially a focus on cost reduction is common (Merchant & Van der Stede 2007, p. 728). This might include a more elaborate cost accounting and less aggregate financial measures – for instance individual cost items – included in the evaluation of managers.

There is empirical evidence that companies of the PMS Design 1 type indeed do use more non-financial measures, for instance from a study among 52 New Zealand manufacturing firms by Hoque (2003, p. 496) and a study among Dutch organisations by Verbeeten (2005, p. 5). However, Verbeeten does not find support for the hypothesis that companies which better align their PMS with their strategy outperform their peers.

(2) Incentives design

Concerning the design of the incentives, the following suggestions are made for companies of the *PMS Design 1 type*: As discussed in the chapter about short-termism, the measurement horizon should be extended. Shank & Govindarajan (1992, pp. 19-20) furthermore propose to define a relatively high proportion of total compensation as variable bonus in order to encourage managers to take greater risks which is necessary to increase market share.[49] Moreover, more reliance should be placed on subjective judgments by superiors since it is hard to measure objectively the long-term effects of effort put into the development of critical success factors. However, this might be inappropriate in a subsidiary controlling context due to the information asymmetry involved.

(3) Planning and control process

In the *PMS Design 1* group, there is a limited possibility to plan in advance and predict targets accurately so that budgets are more of a short-term planning tool rather than a tool for control (Shank & Govindarajan 1992, pp. 17-18). The system in general is more informal and there is a participative decision-making environment instead of a top-down determination of targets. In contrast, in the *PMS Design 2 group*, controls are tighter with an emphasis on budget achievement. Furthermore, procedures are more formal, standardised and centralised (Merchant & Van der Stede 2007, p. 728).

Above, it was shown that build, prospector and differentiating firms require a similar design of PMS. However, it was neglected that there can be several combinations of strategies according to the different typologies. For instance a build firm does not necessarily have to follow a differentiation strategy. Thus there can be conflicting combinations in terms of the type of controls to use. Such trade-offs are difficult to solve unless the strategy can be changed to a consistent combination or the strategy according to one typology is more important so that control systems can be tailored to this dimension (Shank & Govindarajan 1992, p. 22).

---

[49] Note from the author: high variable payments increase the willingness to take risks as managers are compensated for large gains but do not get a "negative bonus" if they make large losses, i.e. they can earn more than they can lose.

5.3.2 Size

5.3.2.1 Introduction

A subsidiary's size can be measured in two ways: Either by its absolute size – for instance measured in number of employees, amount of sales or balance sheet total – or by its relative size compared to the company group as a whole (Borchers 2000, p. 67). Relative size indicates the importance of a subsidiary for the company group, especially if it is calculated by the relation of important financial measures such as profit. Subsequently, however, only absolute size will be analysed as a contextual factor.

Although it is commonly realised that size is an important contextual factor in PMS design, few studies take it into account as a variable (Chenhall 2003, p. 148). Those that do usually refer to the size of a company group as a whole and not to subsidiary size. Integrated PMS approaches were originally developed for and tested in larger companies and might have to be adapted to the smaller size in small and medium-sized enterprises (SME) (Smith & Smith 2007, p. 394). Therefore, subsequently, particularities for the design of PMS in SME are derived from their special characteristics as investigated from literature.

5.3.2.2 Consequences for PMS design

(1) Choice of performance measures

There are a number of constraints that one should be aware of when choosing and designing performance measures for SME: First of all, such companies are likely to gather a smaller amount of quantitative data. Availability is often restricted to financial accounting data; often with a poor allocation of costs to organisational units or processes (Borchers 2000, p. 70). This might impede the use of certain financial and especially non-financial performance measures. Moreover, business processes are likely to be less standardised and formalised and there is less specialisation so that it might not be possible to break down performance measures as far down as in larger companies. Besides that, the use of capital market measures is not possible either as SME are regularly not listed.

Given these constraints and the facts that human resources might be scarce (Smith & Smith 2007, p. 394) and management is often strongly involved in daily operating business, corporate centres should be careful not to ask too much of their small subsidiaries (Borchers 2000, p. 71). This is also in the interest of the corporate centre since it needs to be able to rely on the reported data. It is recommended to confine to few important performance measures and let subsidiary managers participate in the choice in order to make sure that reliable data is available.

SME are regularly considered to be more flexible and adaptive to their environment due to their leaner structures. This is also necessary since they might not be able to drive the market but must react to changes in the market (Smith & Smith 2007, p. 394). This also means that KPI might change more often. Hence, a more frequent review of the measures in use is suggested.

(2) Planning and control process

SME often have less sophisticated internal planning systems in general and engage less in market research activities and external information gathering (Chenhall 2003, p. 148; Borchers 2000, p. 70). Due to the limitations of general planning it might also be hard to plan targets for performance measures. Moreover, it is often stated in literature that employee qualification and management expertise is lower in SME (Smith & Smith 2007, p. 394; Borchers 2000, p. 67). This might imply the danger that integrated PMS are implemented deficiently if done by subsidiary management which is reinforced by the lack of resources in the subsidiaries.

Therefore, a stronger intervention in the process of performance target planning by corporate management is recommended in SME.

6 Conclusion

In this thesis, it was shown how subsidiaries can be controlled with the help of PMS. A main part of the thesis was dedicated to systematically examining financial measures. The conclusion drawn from the analysis was that no measure alone can fulfil all the requirements so that several financial measures should be combined. Furthermore, it turned out that the dysfunctions and biases inherent in financial measures cannot be completely eliminated, so that a combination with non-financial measures was recommended. Furthermore, the estimation of betas of unlisted subsidiaries was discussed, supplemented by a case study in the Appendix.

Another core statement of the thesis was that PMS should be integrated with the other management systems of the company and its strategy. Latter can especially be achieved by operationalising strategy two-dimensionally.

After discussing theory and methodology of contingency theory, contextual factors which influence the design of PMS were pointed out. It was argued that PMS should be designed both company group-specific and subsidiary-specific. In terms of the contingency approach, the thesis' overview character should be kept in mind when deriving recommendations for practice. Implementing a contingency approach in practice requires the simultaneous consideration of a large number of factors.

This thesis is a first attempt to comprehensively integrate German subsidiary controlling with Anglo-Saxon PMS theory. For a future discussion, it will be especially important that unambiguous definitions and demarcations of the core terminology and concepts are established. A sub-topic which was left out due to its large scale but which is of particular interest in contemporary company groups is specific problems in multinational subsidiary controlling. Furthermore, the thesis could be complemented by the discussion of synergy effects and transfer pricing issues.

List of appendices

Appendix 1: Aggregation of EVA and REVA

	SBUs		CORPORATE			AGGREGATION RULE
	SBU 1	SBU 2	aggregation	independent calculation	consistent?	
β	1.0	2.0	1.33	1.33		average weighted by MV of equity
					yes	
market return	15.0%	15.0%	15.0%	15.0%	yes	equal
risk free return	5.0%	5.0%	5.0%	5.0%	yes	equal
return on eq.	15.0%	25.0%	18.3%	18.3%		average weighted by MV of equity
					yes	
return on debt	5.0%	5.0%	5.0%	5.0%	yes	equal
MV equity	100.0	50.0	150.0	150.0	yes	sum
MV debt	100.0	100.0	200.0	200.0	yes	sum
Σ market value	200.0	150.0	350.0	350.0	yes	sum
WACC	10.0%	11.7%	10.7%	10.7%		average weighted by total MV
					yes	
NOPAT	25.0	20.0	45.0	45.0	yes	sum
NA	150.0	80.0	230.0	230.0	yes	sum
EVA	10.0	10.7	20.7	20.4	! no !	sum
REVA	5.0	2.5	7.5	7.5	yes	sum

Source: Own calculation

The calculation above shows that EVA cannot be aggregated to the corporate level by simply summing it up from the subsidiaries. This is illustrated in the table by aggregating all the components and comparing the results with the result of an independent calculation on the corporate level. It turns out that for all components and for REVA the aggregation is equal to the independent calculation, but not for EVA.

The reason is that in the components of EVA there are two different proportions of SBU values: market value proportions in the WACC and NA proportions in the calculation of EVA. For SBU1, it is shown below that the proportions are not equal by dividing the respective SBU value by the respective total value:

$$\frac{NA_i}{total\ NA} = \frac{market\ value_i}{total\ market\ value}$$

$$\frac{150}{230} \neq \frac{200}{350}$$

So why is this a problem concerning aggregation? Below, the separate calculations of EVA for the SBUs is shown:

$$EVA = NOPAT - WACC * NA$$
$$EVA_{SBU1} = 25.0 - 10.0\% * 150$$
$$EVA_{SBU2} = 20.0 - 11.7\% * 80$$

If the equations are summed up for the corporate level, the following equation results:

$$EVA_{Corporate,aggregated} = (25.0 - 10\% * 150) + (20.0 - 11.7\% * 80)$$

Once the equation is rearranged, the problem can be seen: The WACC is now weighted by the NA values although it should be weighted by the market values:

$$EVA_{Corporate,aggregated} = (25.0 + 20.0) - (10\% * 150 + 11.7\% * 80)$$

Appendix 2: Age bias with alternating CF

	Period		1	2	3	4	5	6
	CF	-1000	250	200	250	200	250	200
Accounting / EVA	NA beginning		1000	833	667	500	333	167
	Depreciation (straight-line)		-167	-167	-167	-167	-167	-167
	Profit (CF - Depr.)		83	33	83	33	83	33
	Return		8%	4%	13%	7%	25%	20%
	Residual Income (EVA)		-11	-46	20	-14	52	18
	Discounted EVA (Σ=MVA)		-10	-38	15	-10	33	10
CFROI mod.	Gross Inv		1000	1000	1000	1000	1000	1000
	Ec. Depr.		-131	-131	-131	-131	-131	-131
	CF - Ec. Depr.		119	69	119	69	119	69
	CFROI		12%	7%	12%	7%	12%	7%
	Residual Income (CVA)		24	-26	24	-26	24	-26
Economic depreciation	PV beginning		1000	845	725	544	395	183
	PV end		845	725	544	395	183	0
	Ec. Depr.		-155	-120	-181	-148	-213	-183
	Ec. Income (CF - Ec. Depr.)		95	80	69	52	37	17
	Ec. Return		9%	9%	9%	9%	9%	9%
	Residual Income		0	0	0	0	0	0
Sinking-fund depreciation	Capital base (beginning)		1000	869	725	568	395	207
	Annuity		-226	-226	-226	-226	-226	-226
	thereof capital charge		-95	-82	-69	-54	-37	-20
	thereof depreciation		-131	-144	-157	-172	-189	-207
	Profit		119	56	93	28	61	-7
	Return		12%	6%	13%	5%	16%	-3%
	Residual Income		24	-26	24	-26	24	-26

Source: Own calculation

The calculation above is based on CF alternating between 250 and 200. The reason for using alternating CF is the following: If monotonically increasing CF were chosen, it could not be clearly seen whether EVA increases due to the increasing CF or due to the age bias. The results are as follows:

➤ As CF fluctuates, CFROI also fluctuates. However, for equal CFs in different periods, CFROI is also equal. Hence, there is no age bias. The same is true for sinking-fund depreciation.

➤ In traditional accounting, there is age bias. EVA for equal CFs increases with time.

➢ Economic depreciation reports constant residual income although CF changes.

Appendix 3: Derivation of (un-)levering formula

$$\beta_{assets} = \frac{D}{D+E}\beta_{debt} + \frac{E}{D+E}\beta_{equity} \qquad\qquad | -\frac{D}{D+E}\beta_{debt} \qquad | \text{ switch}$$

sides

$$\frac{E}{D+E}\beta_{equity} = \beta_{assets} - \frac{D}{D+E}\beta_{debt} \qquad\qquad |/\left(\frac{E}{D+E}\right)$$

$$\beta_{equity} = \frac{D+E}{E}\beta_{assets} - \frac{D}{E}\beta_{debt}$$

$$\beta_{equity} = \frac{D}{E}\beta_{assets} + \frac{E}{E}\beta_{assets} - \frac{D}{E}\beta_{debt}$$

$$\beta_{equity} = \beta_{assets} + \frac{D}{E}(\beta_{assets} - \beta_{debt}) \qquad\qquad | \text{ assuming that } \beta_{debt} = 0$$

$$\beta_{equity} = \beta_{assets} + \frac{D}{E}\beta_{assets}$$

$$\beta_{equity} = \beta_{assets}\left(1 + \frac{D}{E}\right)$$

Appendix 4: Case Study (beta estimation)

A. Introduction

Subsequently, the beta of the German car manufacturer BMW Group will be calculated according to the comparable company approach (CCA). As BMW shares are listed, beta can be calculated directly from financial market data as well. Therefore, in practice the CCA would not be applied. However, this provides the opportunity to compare the result of the CCA calculation with the one of a normal beta calculation.

The financial market data used was retrieved from http://finance.yahoo.com, the other company data was taken from the respective consolidated IFRS annual reports 2009.

B. Comparable company approach

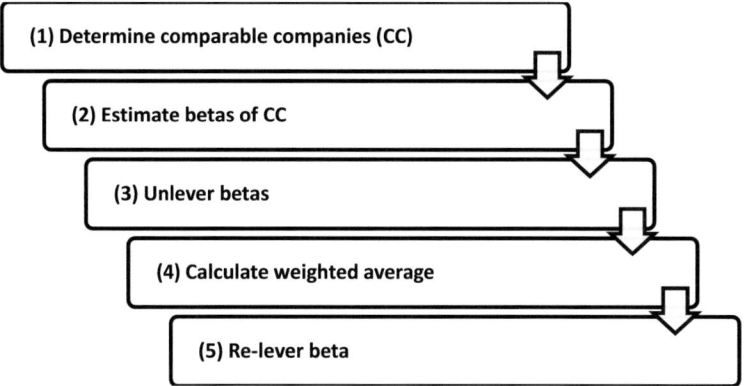

(1) Determine comparable companies (CC)

(2) Estimate betas of CC

(3) Unlever betas

(4) Calculate weighted average

(5) Re-lever beta

(1) <u>Determine comparable companies</u>

An industry beta is calculated, i.e. companies from the same sector are considered in the calculation. The analysis is confined to car manufacturers in the Euro-zone in order to avoid currency effects, namely Fiat, Daimler and Renault.

Volkswagen and Peugeot are treated as statistical outliers and therefore not considered since they are expected to distort the result of the calculation. Volkswagen share price was extraordinarily affected by the Porsche take-over in 2008. Peugeot shares were massively depreciated during the last three years which results in a market value of equity being only approximately half the book value so that the leverage calculated by market values is extremely high which influences results in the calculation of the un-levered beta.

(2) Estimate betas of CC

The calculations are based on weekly logarithmic returns of five years (2005 to 2009). The reason for using weekly returns instead of daily returns is that this reduces noise in the statistics.

The Stoxx Euro 600 index which comprises 315 shares is used as a proxy for the market portfolio.

Date	Euro Stoxx		Fiat		Daimler		...
	index	In-return	price	In-return	price	In-return	...
28.12.2009	274.78	0.35%	10.07	0.10%	37.23	-0.51%	...
21.12.2009	273.82	2.53%	10.06	0.80%	37.42	1.83%	...
14.12.2009	266.97	0.30%	9.98	-0.50%	36.74	4.31%	...
07.12.2009	266.17	-1.77%	10.03	-3.43%	35.19	-2.03%	...
30.11.2009	270.93	2.79%	10.38	7.09%	35.91	3.66%	...
...	...	...	...	...	...	...	

In the table below, the results of the analysis can be seen. The standard deviation and covariance have been calculated with the Excel formulas COVAR(...) and STDEVA(...). Volatility is the standard definition multiplied by the square root of 52 in order to translate it from weekly standard deviation to an annualised measure according to the so-called square-root-of-time rule (Daníelsson & Zigrand 2005, p. 1). R-squared is the squared correlation coefficient of the respective share and Euro Stoxx. The levered beta is calculated by dividing the respective covariance by the squared standard deviation of Euro Stoxx's returns.

	Euro Stoxx	Fiat	Daimler	Renault
standard dev. (sd)	3.29%	6.41%	5.73%	6.85%
volatility	23.72%	46.24%	41.29%	49.41%
cov w/ Euro Stoxx		0.14%	0.15%	0.19%
r-squared		0.45	0.61	0.68
β levered		1.31	1.36	1.71

The interpretation of the data is shown exemplarily for Fiat: Beta is 1.31, i.e. for each percent that Euro Stoxx moves, Fiat is expected to move by 1.31 percent. 45 percent of Fiat's total volatility can be explained by the general market movement.

(3) Unlever betas + (4) Calculate weighted average

In the lower part of the table below (shaded in light blue), the betas calculated above are unlevered with the formula displayed below and weighted by their market capitalisation.

$$\beta_{unlevered} = \frac{\beta_{levered}}{\left(1 + \frac{D}{E}\right)}$$

The upper part of the table is needed to calculate the leverage. Equity is the number of shares times the share price. Debt is calculated in a simplified way by deducting (book) equity from the balance sheet total, i.e. it also includes provisions.

	Fiat	Daimler	Renault
no. of shares	1,237,000,000	1,024,000,000	285,000,000
share price 31/12/2009	10.07 €	37.23 €	36.20 €
equity (market cap.)	12,456,590,000	38,123,520,000	10,317,000,000
debt (book value)	56,120,000,000	96,994,000,000	47,506,000,000
leverage (debt/equity)	4.51	2.54	4.60
β levered	1.31	1.36	1.71
β unlevered	0.24	0.38	0.31
β unlevered (weighted average)	0.34		

(5) Re-lever beta

As a last step, the unlevered beta is re-levered with BMW's leverage according to the same principle as it was unlevered above. The resulting beta is 1.80.

	BMW
no. of shares	602,000,000
share price	31.80 €
equity (market value)	19,143,600,000
debt (book value)	82,038,000,000
leverage (debt/equity)	4.29
β re-levered	1.80

C. Regular calculation of BMW equity beta and comparison

Below, the analysis of BMW's stock market data can be seen. Its 'real' beta is only 1.06 which is substantially different from the beta of 1.80 according to the CCA. However, the comparison of BMW's volatility shows, that it is extraordinarily low compared to its peers.

	BMW
standard dev. (sd)	4.86%
volatility	35.02%
cov w/ Euro Stoxx	0.11%
r-squared	0.51
β levered	1.06

D. Conclusion

The following conclusion can be drawn from the case study: It is relatively simple to calculate betas according to the CCA. However, the comparison with the actual equity beta shows that the method can be quite unreliable. Furthermore, for the case of BMW it was very easy to determine comparable companies since the sector can be demarcated easily and there are several car manufacturing companies which are listed on the stock market. Besides the question which companies are included in the analysis, there are a number of other decisions that have to be made such as which frequency of returns (daily or weekly) is selected and which period of time is analysed. This creates possibilities of manipulation.

References

Abarbanell, J & Bernard, V 2000, 'Is the U.S. Stock Market Myopic?', *Journal of Accounting Research*, vol 38, no. 2, pp. 221-242.

Abernethy, M, Bouwens, J & Van Lent, L 2004, 'Determinants of Control System Design in Divisionalized Firms', *The Accounting Review*, vol 79, no. 3, pp. 545-570.

Anthony, RN 1973, 'Accounting for the cost of equity', *Harvard Business Review*, vol Nov/Dec, pp. 88-102.

Anthony, RN & Govindarajan, V 2001, *Management Control Systems*, 10th edn, Boston.

Ballou, B, Heitger, D & Donnell, L 2010, 'Creating Effective Dashboards. How companies can improve executive decision making and board oversight.', *Strategic Finance*, vol 91, no. 1, pp. 27-32.

Ballwieser, W 2007, *Unternehmensbewertung. Prozeß, Methoden und Probleme.*, 2nd edn, Stuttgart.

Bititci, US, Carrie, AS & McDevitt, L 1997, 'Integrated performance measurement systems: a development guide', *International Journal of Operations & Production Management*, vol 17, no. 5, pp. 522-534.

Bititci, US, Mendibil, K, Nudurupati, S, Garengo, P & Turner, T 2006, 'Dynamics of performance measurement and organisational culture', *International Journal of Operations & Production Management*, vol 26, no. 12, pp. 1325-1350.

Bititci, US, Nudurupati, SS & Turner, TJ 2002, 'Web-enabled performance measurement systems. Management implications.', *International Journal of Operations & Production Management*, vol 22, no. 11, pp. 1273-1287.

Black, A & Fraser, P 2000, 'Stock market short-termism - an international perspective', *Journal of Multinational Financial Management*, vol 12, pp. 135-158.

Bleicher, K 1991, *Organisation. Strategien - Strukturen - Kulturen*, 2nd edn, Wiesbaden.

Bleicher, K 1972, 'Die Entwicklung eines systemorientierten Organisations- und Führungsmodells der Unternehmung', in Bleicher, K (ed): *Schriftenreihe Organisation und Führung. Band I: Organisation als System*, Wiesbaden.

Borchers, S 2000, *Beteiligungscontrolling in der Managementholding: ein integratives Konzept*, Wiesbaden.

Borchers, S 2006, 'Beteiligungscontrolling - Ein Überblick', *Zeitschrift für Planung & Unternehmenssteuerung*, vol 17, pp. 233-250.

Borgman, RH & Strong, RH 2006, 'Growth Rate and Implied Beta: Interactions of Cost of Capital Models', *Journal of Business & Economic Studies*, vol 12, no. 1, pp. 1-11.

Bowman, RG & Bush, SR 2006, 'Using Comparable Companies to Estimate the Betas of Private Companies', *Journal of Applied Finance*, vol 16, no. 2, pp. 71-81.

Brailsford, T, Heaney, R & Bilson, C 2006, *Investments. Concepts and Applications.*, 3rd edn, Melbourne.

Brealey, R, Myers, S & Allen, F 2008, *Principles of corporate finance*, 9th edn, The McGraw-Hill Companies.

Brignall, STJ 2007, 'A financial perspective on performance measurement', *The Irish Accounting Review*, vol 14, no. 1, pp. 15-29.

Britzelmaier, B 2009, *Kompakt-Training Wertorientierte Unternehmensführung*, Ludwigshafen (Rhein).

Britzelmaier, B 2010, 'Company valuation in Emerging Markets', *Pforzheim University Working Paper*.

Broadbent, J & Laughlin, R 2009, 'Performance management systems: a conceptual model', *Management Accounting Research*, vol 20, pp. 283-295.

Burger, A & Ulbrich, PR 2005, *Beteiligungscontrolling*, München.

Chenhall, RH 2006, 'The contingent design of performance measures', in *Contemporary Issues in Management Accounting*, Oxford, New York.

Chenhall, RH 2005, 'Integrative strategic performance measurement systems, strategic alignment of manufacturing, learning and strategic outcomes: an exploratory study', *Accounting, Organizations and Society*, vol 30, pp. 395-422.

Chenhall, RH 2003, 'Management control systems design within its organizational context: findings from contingency-based reseach and directions for the future', *Accounting, Organizations and Society*, vol 28, pp. 127-168.

Chow, CW & Van der Stede, WA 2006, 'The Use and Usefulness of Nonfinancial Performance Measures', *Management Accounting Quarterly*, vol 7, no. 3, pp. 1-8.

Damodaran, A 2010, *The Dark Side of Valuation: Valuing Young, Distressed, and Complex Businesses*, 2nd edn, Upper Saddle River.

Daníelsson, J & Zigrand, J-P 2005, 'On time-scaling of risk and the square-root-of-time rule', *EFA 2004 Maastricht Meetings Paper No. 5339, available via Social Science Research Network (SSRN)*.

Dieck, RH 2007, *Measurement Uncertainty. Methods and Applications*, 4th edn, Research Triangle Park.

Dittmar, C 2004, *Knowledge Warehouse. Ein integrativer Ansatz des Organisationsgedächtnisses und die computergestützte Umsetzung auf Basis des Data Warehouse-Konzepts*, Wiesbaden.

Drucker, P 1969, *The Age of Discontinuity: Guidelines to Our Changing Society*, New York.

Drury, C 2004, *Management and cost accounting*, 6th edn, London.

Eling, M & Schuhmacher, F 2007, 'Does the choice of performance measure influence the evaluation of hedge funds?', *Journal of Banking & Finance*, vol 31, pp. 2632-2647.

Erasmus, PD & Lambrechts, IJ 2006, 'EVA and CFROI: A comparative analysis', *Management Dynamics*, vol 15, no. 1, pp. 14-26.

Ewert, R & Wagenhofer, A 2000, 'Rechnungslegung und Kennzahlen für das wertorientierte Management', in Ewert, R (ed) & Wagenhofer, A (ed): *Wertorientiertes Management. Konzepte und Umsetzungen zur Unternehmenswertsteigerung*, Stuttgart.

Ewert, R & Wagenhofer, A 2008, *Interne Unternehmensrechnung*, 7th edn, Heidelberg.

Fama, EF & French, KR 1993, 'Common risk factors in the returns on stocks and bonds', *Journal of Financial Economics*, vol 33, no. 1, pp. 3-56.

Fama, EF & French, KR 2004, 'The Capital Asset Pricing Model: Theory and Evidence', *Journal of Economic Perspectives*, vol 18, no. 3, pp. 25-46.

Faul, K 2004, *Wertorientiertes Controlling. Ein Ansatz zur Unternehmens- und Verhaltenssteuerung in dezentralen Organisationen.*, Hamburg.

Fernández, P 2003, 'Levered and Unlevered Beta', *IESE Business School (University of Navarra) Working Paper no. 488*, http://www.iese.edu/research/pdfs/DI-0488-E.pdf.

Fischer, BR 2001, *Performanceanalyse in der Praxis*, 2nd edn, Oldenbourg, München.

Fuchs, H 1972, 'Systemtheorie', in Bleicher, K (ed): *Schriftenreihe Organisation und Führung. Band I: Organisation als System*, Wiesbaden.

Gabler Wirtschaftslexikon 2010, *Integration*, http://wirtschaftslexikon.gabler.de/Definition/integration.html.

Garvey, GT & Milbourn, TT 2000, 'EVA versus Earnings: Does It Matter Which Is More Highly Correlated with Stock Returns?', *Journal of Accounting Research*, vol 38, pp. 209-245.

Gebhard, WR, Lee, CM & Swaminathan, B 2001, 'Toward an Implied Cost of Capital', *Journal of Accounting Research*, vol 39, no. 1, pp. 135-176.

Gladen, W 2008, *Performance Measurement: Controlling mit Kennzahlen*, 4th edn, Wiesbaden.

Gleich, R 2001, *Das System des Performance Measurement. Theoretisches Grundkonzept, Entwicklungs- und Anwendungsstand.*, München.

Grünig, M 2002, *Performance-Measurement-Systeme: Messung und Steuerung von Unternehmensleistung*, Wiesbaden.

Hitt, MA, Ireland, RD & Hoskisson, RE 2007, *Strategic management: competitiveness and globalization*, 7th edn, Mason.

Hoffjan, A 2009, *Internationales Controlling*, Stuttgart.

Hoffjan, A & Weide, G 2006, 'Organisation des internationalen Controlling - Im Spannungsfeld zwischen Standardisierung und Differenzierung', *Die Unternehmung*, vol 60, no. 6, pp. 389-406.

Holler, A 2009, *New Metrics for Value-Based Management. Enhancement of Performance Measurement and Empirical Evidence on Value-Relevance.*, Wiesbaden.

Hoque, Z 2003, *Strategic Management Accounting: Concepts, Processes and Issues*, Frenchs Forest.

Hoque, Z 2004, 'A contingency model of the association between strategy, environmental uncertainty and performance measurement', *International Business Review*, vol 13, pp. 485-502.

Horváth, P 1997, 'Internationales Beteiligungscontrolling. Das Controllingthema für die kommenden Jahre.', *Controller Magazin*, vol 2, pp. 81-88.

Horváth, P 2006, *Controlling*, 10th edn, München.

Huch, B, Behme, W & Ohlendorf, T 2004, *Rechnungswesen-orientiertes Controlling*, 4th edn, Heidelberg.

Hüllmann, U 2003, *Wertorientiertes Controlling für eine Management-Holding*, München.

Jackson, MC 2000, *System approaches to management*, New York.

Jalbert, T & Landry, SP 2003, 'Which Performance Measurement Is Best for Your Company?', *Management Accounting Quarterly*, vol 4, no. 3, pp. 32-41.

Jensen, MC & Meckling, WH 1976, 'Theory of the Firm: Managerial Behavior, Agency Costs and Ownership Structure', *Journal of Financial Economics*, vol 3, pp. 305-360.

Jensen, MC & Meckling, WH 2009, 'Specific Knowledge and Divisional Performance Measurement', *Journal of Applied Corporate Finance*, vol 21, no. 2, pp. 49-57.

Jorion, P 2001, *Value-at-risk. The new benchmark for managing financial risk*, New York.

Kaplan, R & Norton, D 2001, *The Strategy Focused Organization*, Boston.

Kennerley, M & Neely, A 2003, 'Measuring performance in a changing business environment', *International Journal of Operations & Production Management*, vol 23, no. 2, pp. 213-229.

Kieser, A & Kubicek, H 1992, *Organisation*, 3rd edn, Berlin.

Kieser, A & Walgenbach, P 2007, *Organisation*, 5th edn, Stuttgart.

Koller, T, Goedhart, M & Wessels, D 2005, *Valuation. Measuring and managing the value of companies.*, 4th edn, New Jersey.

König, E 2005, 'Das Systemmodell der Personalen Systemtheorie', in König, E (ed) & Volmer, G (ed): *Systemisch denken und handeln. Personale Systemtheorie in Erwachsenenbildung und Organisationsberatung.*, Weinheim/Basel.

Kremer, P 2008, *Konzerncontrolling. Ein unternehmenswertorientierter und beteiligungsspezifischer Ansatz.*, Berlin.

Krotter, S 2008, *Performance-Messung, Erwartungsänderungen und Analystenschätzungen. Theoretische Konzeption und empirische Umsetzung.*, Frankfurt am Main.

Krupp, A 2007, *Beteiligungscontrolling kompakt*, Norderstedt.

Kruschwitz, L 2007, *Investitionsrechnung*, 11th edn, München.

Küpper, H-U 2008, *Controlling. Konzeption, Aufgaben, Instrumente.*, 5th edn, Stuttgart.

Küting, K & Eidel, U 1999, 'Performance-Messung und Unternehmensbewertung auf Basis des EVA', *Die Wirtschaftsprüfung*, vol 52, no. 21, pp. 829-838.

Langfield-Smith, K, Thorne, H & Hilton, R 2009, *Management accounting: information for creating and managing value*, 5th edn, North Ryde, NSW, Australia.

Langguth, H 2008, *Kapitalmarktorientiertes Wertmanagement*, München.

Laverty, KJ 1996, 'Economic "short-termism": the debate, the unresolved issues, and the implications for management practice and research', *Academy of Management Review*, vol 21, no. 3, pp. 825-860.

Laverty, KJ 2004, 'Managerial myopia or systematic short-termism? The importance of managerial systems in valuing the long term.', *Management Decision*, vol 42, no. 8, pp. 949-962.

Lebas, M & Euske, K 2007, 'A conceptual and operational delineation of performance', in *Business performance measurement: Unifying theory and integrating practice*, Cambridge.

Lintner, J 1965, 'The Valuation of Risk Assets and the Selection of Risky Investments in Stock Portfolios and', *The Review of Economics and Statistics*, vol 47, no. 1, pp. 13-37.

Littkemann, J 2009, 'Einführung in das Beteiligungscontrolling', in Littkemann, J (ed): *Beteiligungscontrolling. Ein Handbuch für die Unternehmens- und Beratungspraxis. Band I: Grundlagen, sowie bilanzielle, steuerliche und sonstige rechtliche Aspekte des Beteiligungscontrollings.*, 2nd edn, Herne.

Littkemann, J 2009a, 'Managementorientierte Ausrichtung des Beteiligungscontrollings', in Littkemann, J (ed): *Beteiligungscontrolling. Ein Handbuch für die Unternehmens- und Beratungspraxis. Band I: Grundlagen, sowie bilanzielle, steuerliche und sonstige rechtliche Aspekte des Beteiligungscontrollings.*, 2nd edn, Herne.

Littkemann, J & Derfuß, K 2009, 'Verhaltensorientierte Ausrichtung des Beteiligungscontrollings', in Littkemann, J (ed): *Beteiligungscontrolling. Ein Handbuch für die Unternehmens- und Beratungspraxis*, 2nd edn.

Lucey, T 2003, *Management Accounting*, 5th edn, New York.

Maier, SC 2001, *Beteiligungscontrolling in deutschen Unternehmen: Kontextfaktoren, Systemtypen, Performance*, Frankfurt.

Marginson, D & McAulay, L 2008, 'Exploring the debate on short-termism: a theoretical and empirical analysis', *Strategic Management Journal*, vol 29, pp. 273-292.

Markowitz, H 1952, 'Portfolio Selection', *Journal of Finance*, vol 7, no. 1, pp. pp. 71-91.

Matschke, MJ & Brösel, G 2007, *Unternehmensbewertung. Funktionen - Methoden - Grundsätze.*, 3rd edn, Wiesbaden.

McLaney, E 2006, *Business Finance*, 7th edn, Essex.

Meier, H 2001, *Wertorientiertes Beteiligungs-Controlling*, Wiesbaden.

Merchant, KA & Van der Stede, WA 2007, *Management Control Systems. Performance Measurement, Evaluation and Incentives*, 2nd edn, Essex.

Meyer, C 2007, *Betriebswirtschaftliche Kennzahlen und Kennzahlen-Systeme*, 4th edn, Sternenfels.

Miles, RE, Snow, CC, Myer, AD & Coleman, HJ 1978, 'Organizational Strategy, Structure and Process', *Academy of Management Review*, pp. 546-564.

Mittendorfer, C 2004, 'Value Based Management in der Unternehmenspraxis', in *Handbuch Finanzmanagement in der Praxis*, Wiesbaden.

Morgan, G 1998, *Images of organisations*, Thousand Oaks.

Neely, A, Gregory, M & Platts, K 1995, 'Performance measurement system design', *International Journal of Operations & Production Management*, vol 15, no. 4, pp. 80-116.

O'Byrne, SF 1997, 'EVA® and Shareholder Return', *Financial Practice and Education*, pp. 50-54.

Otley, DT 1980, 'The contingency theory of management accounting: achievement and prognosis', *Accounting, Organizations and Society*, vol 5, no. 4, pp. 413-428.

Otley, D 1999, 'Performance management: a framework for management control systems research', *Management Accounting Research*, vol 10, pp. 363-382.

Perridon, L & Steiner, M 2007, *Finanzwirtschaft der Unternehmung*, 14th edn, Vahlen, München.

Petersen, C, Plenborg, T & Schøler, F 2006, 'Issues in Valuation of Privately Held Firms', *The Journal of Private Equity*, pp. 33-48.

Pfister, C 2003, *Divisionale Kapitalkosten. Theorie und Anwendung*, Bern.

Porter, ME 1985, 'Technology and competitive advantage', *Journal of Business Strategy*, pp. 60-78.

Pratt, SP 2002, *Cost of Capital. Estimation and Applications.*, 2nd edn, New Jersey.

Preißler, PR 2008, *Betriebswirtschaftliche Kennzahlen*, München.

Printz, T 2008, *Performance Measurement. Gestaltung eines Werttreibersystems.*, Hamburg.

Riegler, C 2000, 'Anreizsysteme und wertorientiertes Management', in *Wertorientiertes Management. Konzepte und Umsetzungen zur Unternehmenswertsteigerung*, Stuttgart.

Roll, R 1977, 'A Critique of the Asset Pricing Theory's Tests Part I: On Past and Potential Testability of the Theory.', *Journal of Financial Economics*, vol 4, pp. 129-176.

Roll, R & Ross, SA 1984, 'The Arbitrage Pricing Theory Approach to Strategic Portfolio Planning', *Financial Analysts Journal*, pp. 14-26.

Schaefer, OM 2002, *Performance Measures in Value Management. A model based approach to explain the CVA and EVA measures.*, Bielefeld.

Scharfstein, DS & Stein, JC 2000, 'The Dark Side of Internal Capital Markets: Divisional Rent-Seeking and Inefficient Investment', *Journal of Finance*, vol 55, no. 6, pp. 2537-2564.

Schlegel, D 2008, 'The valuation of patents - a comparison of methods', *World Journal of Management and Economics*, vol 2, no. 3, pp. 3-10.

Schmidbauer, R 1998, *Konzeption eines unternehmenswertorientierten Beteiligungs-Controlling im Konzern.*, Frankfurt.

Schreyer, M 2007, *Entwicklung und Implementierung von Performance Measurement Systemen*, Wiesbaden.

Schultze, W & Hirsch, C 2004, *Unternehmenswertsteigerung durch wertorientiertes Controlling. Goodwill-Bilanzierung in der Unternehmenssteuerung.*, München.

Schumacher, T 2005, *Beteiligungscontrolling in der Management-Holding. Optimierung der Rationalitätssicherung durch Nutzung des Eigenkapitalmarktes*, Wiesbaden.

Schumann, J 2008, *Unternehmenswertorientierung in Konzernrechnungslegung und Controlling. Impairment of Assets (IAS 36) im Kontext bereichsbezogener Unternehmensbewertung und Performancemessung*, Wiesbaden.

Shank, J & Govindarajan, V 1992, 'Strategic cost management: Tailoring controls to strategies', *Journal of Cost Management*, pp. 14-24.

Sharpe, WF 1964, 'Capital Asset Prices: A Theory of Market Equilibrium under Conditions of Risk', *Journal of Finance*, vol 19, no. 3, pp. 425-442.

Shiller, RJ 2003, 'From Efficient Markets Theory to Behavioral Finance', *Journal of Economic Perspectives*, vol 17, no. 1, pp. 83-104.

Simons, R 2000, *Performance measurement and control systems for implementing strategy*, Upper Saddle River.

Smith, MH & Smith, D 2007, 'Implementing strategically aligned performance measurement in small firms', *International Journal of Production Economics*, vol 106, pp. 393-408.

Spitzer, DR 2007, *Transforming Performance Measurement: Rethinking the Way We Measure and Drive Organizational Success*, New York.

Staehle, WH, Conrad, P & Sydow, J 1999, *Management. Eine verhaltenswissenschaftliche Perspektive.*, 8th edn, München.

Steiner, M & Bruns, C 2002, *Wertpapiermanagement. Professionelle Wertpapieranalyse und Portfoliostrukturierung.*, 8th edn, Stuttgart.

Stern, JM, Stewart, BGI & Chew, DHJ 1996, 'EVA: An integrated financial management system', *European Financial Management*, vol 2, no. 2, pp. 223-245.

Tangen, S 2004, 'Performance measurement: from philosophy to practice', *International Journal of Productivity and Performance Management*, vol 53, no. 8, pp. 726-737.

Trützschler, K, Tomaszweski, C & Blome, M 2007, 'Die Auswirkungen einer IFRS-Umstellung auf strategische Steuerungs- und Finanzkennzahlen', in Heyd, R (ed) & Von Keitz, I (ed): *IFRS-Management. Interessenschutz auf dem Prüfstand. Treffsichere Unternehmensbeurteilung. Konsequenzen für das Management*, München.

Verbeeten, FHM 2005, "New' Performance Measures: Determinants of Their Use and Their Impact on Performance', *Erasmus Research*

Institute of Management Working Paper, Available via Social Science Research Network (SSRN).

Vogel, J 1998, *Marktwertorientiertes Beteiligungscontrolling. Shareholder Value als Maß der Konzernsteuerung.*, Wiesbaden.

Weber, J, Bramsemann, U, Heineke, C & Hirsch, B 2004, *Wertorientierte Unternehmenssteuerung*, Wiesbaden.

Weber, J & Schäffer, U 2006, *Einführung in das Controlling*, 11th edn, Stuttgart.

Weißenberger, BE 2007, *IFRS für Controller*, München.

Wessels, WJ 2000, *Economics*, New York.

Wunderer, R 2007, *Führung und Zusammenarbeit. Eine unternehmerische Führungslehre*, 7th edn, Köln.

Young, DS & O'Byrne, SF 2001, *EVA and Value-based Management. A Practical Guide to Implementation*, New York.